FIN KENNEDY

Fin is a graduate of the MA Writing for Performance programme at Goldsmiths College, London. His first play, *Protection*, was produced at Soho Theatre in 2003, where he was also Pearson writer-in-residence. His second play, *How to Disappear Completely and Never Be Found*, won the 38th Arts Council John Whiting Award, the first time in forty years that an unproduced play had won. It was subsequently commissioned by Samuel West for Sheffield Crucible and enjoyed a sell-out run, transferring to London in 2008. It has also been produced in Australia, New Zealand and the United States, and is becoming a firm favourite with amateur and student groups around the UK.

Fin's first play for teenagers, *Locked In*, a hip-hop musical about pirate radio, was produced by Half Moon Young People's Theatre in 2006 and 2008, and toured nationally. His second play for Half Moon, *We Are Shadows*, toured during autumn 2007. 2008 also saw Fin's first radio commission, *Caesar Price Our Lord*, for BBC Radio 4, which was transmitted in September of that year.

For the past five years he has been writer-in-residence at Mulberry School for Girls in Tower Hamlets, London, where he is co-founder of Mulberry Theatre Company, for whom he wrote *Mehndi Night* (2007), *Stolen Secrets* (2008) and *The Unravelling* (2009) which all premiered at the Edinburgh Fringe Festival. *The Urban Girl's Guide to Camping* premiered at Southwark Playhouse in 2010.

As well as writing plays, Fin also has many years of experience teaching playwrighting at secondary, sixth-form, undergraduate and postgraduate levels. He has worked for schools, youth clubs, local authorities and theatre education teams in inner London and beyond, and is also a visiting lecturer at Goldsmiths College and Boston University.

Other Titles in the Series

Fin Kennedy

PROTECTION

NICK HERN BOOKS
London
www.nickhernbooks.co.uk

A Nick Hern Book

Protection first published in Great Britain in 2003 as a paperback original by Nick Hern Books Limited, 14 Larden Road, London W3 7ST

Reprinted 2008, 2010, 2011, 2012

Protection copyright © 2003 Fin Kennedy

Fin Kennedy has asserted his moral right to be identified as the author of this work

Typeset by Country Setting, Kingsdown, Kent CT14 8ES
Printed in the UK by Mimeo Ltd, Huntingdon, Cambridgeshire PE29 6XX

A CIP catalogue record for this book is available from the British Library

ISBN 978 1 85459 763 2

Woodland CARBON
www.woodlandcarbon.co.uk
NICK HERN BOOKS
Printed on Carbon Captured paper

Author's Note

Protection is a piece of social commentary.

There is of course the argument that all plays are social commentary of one form or other. But what I specifically set out to do with mine was to investigate the workings of an institution whose very name suggests that some sort of publicly funded Service to Society is going on amongst us.

I'm the son of two social workers. I grew up observing the effect of the work on the professionals involved. But in researching the subject as an adult, the more I came to realise that I had been surrounded by something unique. Here, in the midst of western capitalism, was a system whose currency was people, feelings and relationships. As if that wasn't enough, it operated in a climate of high stakes and intense hostility. I wanted to discover what it was that gave these people the strength to keep going, when even those they were trying to help reviled them. Most social workers I met told me that it is because they care. They said it quietly and apologetically, because it is unfashionable and embarrassing to admit.

I am glad there are people in the world who care. It makes them vulnerable, because they have to operate on an intensely personal level to make up for the shortfall in their organisation's resources. But if they operate with integrity, they are afforded a rare opportunity to work with the truth about others, and themselves. When it works, they can claim to be going to the heart of the human spirit.

Social commentary on this macro level appears to have become unfashionable amongst writers of my generation. This troubles me. It is as essential a part of a democracy as a free press. In the current climate of increased centralisation of power, it has become nothing short of urgent. It is also a genre at which theatre excels. I'd like to think it offers a social service of its own. I hope that this play goes some way towards reviving the tradition.

Fin Kennedy

Protection was first performed at Soho Theatre, London, on 3 July 2003, with the following cast:

ANGELA	Saira Todd
ADAM / JEFF	Joe Armstrong
SHIRLEY	Corinne Skinner Carter
GRACE	Lucy Davenport
DAMIEN	Matthew Delamere
DAWN	Margot Leicester
ADELE / JANINE / MANDY	Kellie Shirley
GORDON / DOCTOR	Martin Turner

Director   Abigail Morris
Designer   Tom Piper
Lighting Designer   Jason Taylor
Sound Designer   Matt McKenzie
Costume Designer   Penny Challen

For my mother, with love

Characters

DAWN, *fifty-five, social services team manager*
SHIRLEY, *sixty, social worker*
ANGELA, *thirty-five, social worker*
DAMIEN, *thirty, social worker*
GRACE, *twenty-four, social work trainee*

GORDON, *forty-five, their boss*

ADELE, *twenty-four, Grace's friend*
JEFF, *thirty-five, Angela's friend*

JANINE, *fifteen, client*
ADAM, *fifteen, client*
MANDY, *twenty-five, ex-client*

DOCTOR

*If required, doubling of parts can occur as follows, to make
a total cast of eight:*

Gordon/Shirley – Doctor
Adam – Jeff
Janine – Adele – Mandy

*The action takes place amongst a Family Support Social
Services Team in a British inner city.*

*All London place names are arbitrary and may be changed
accordingly.*

*NB: the social workers are white – except for Shirley, who is
Dominican.*

*A slash (/) in the text indicates the point of interruption by the
following speaker.*

1.

Large office.

DAWN, DAMIEN, ANGELA, SHIRLEY, GRACE *and*
GORDON. *Each of them talks into a phone.*

More phones ring in the background.

DAWN. Good morning, Dawn Talbot.

DAMIEN. Afternoon – sorry morning – Family Services.

ANGELA. Hello yes, Family Support.

SHIRLEY. Children and Families, Shirley here.

GRACE. Hello, Family Support?

GORDON. What? I'm busy.

ALL. Uh-huh.

DAWN. Maybe. Just calm down.

DAMIEN. Yes. It's under control.

ANGELA. Yes. Absolutely, yes.

SHIRLEY. Of course. I'll re-schedule.

GRACE. Don't know. Can I put you on hold?

GORDON. No. Absolutely not.

DAWN. I understand all that.

DAMIEN. So hang on let me get this straight.

ANGELA. Of course I understand, it's obvious.

SHIRLEY. I understand entirely.

GRACE. I don't quite understand.

GORDON. Well they wouldn't understand would they?

ALL. You see, the issue here is –

DAWN. – what we can do under the circumstances.

DAMIEN. – my own feelings on the case.

ANGELA. – a question of accountability.

SHIRLEY. – how you approach the situation.

GRACE. – whether or not I can find him.

GORDON. – other people's incompetence.

ALL. Mm-hm. Well that's not –

DAWN. – the best way forward for my team.

DAMIEN. – been run past *me*.

ANGELA. – the way *I* see it.

SHIRLEY. – going to be a problem.

GRACE. – really been explained to me.

GORDON. – the sort of outfit we're running here.

ALL. Of course, if it was left up to me I'd –

DAWN. – ask for more support.

DAMIEN. – keep it quiet.

ANGELA. – complain to my MP.

SHIRLEY. – happily do that.

GRACE. – put her needs first.

GORDON. – get rid of the lot of them.

ALL. Butt unfortunately it's not.

DAWN. Right then.

DAMIEN. I'm off.

ANGELA. Absolutely.

SHIRLEY. Take care.

GRACE. Sorry.

GORDON. Cheerio.

   They hang up.

   They call to each other.

GRACE. Damien!

DAMIEN. Dawn!

ANGELA. Dawn!

SHIRLEY. Dawn!

DAWN. Gordon!

GORDON. Christ!

Their phones ring again. They all answer them, except for
GORDON, *whose phone keeps ringing.*

DAWN. Dawn Talbot.

DAMIEN. Family Services.

ANGELA. Family Support.

SHIRLEY. Children and Families.

GRACE. Family Support?

GORDON. Can you get that?

Black out.

2.

DAWN*'s office.*

DAWN *with* ANGELA.

DAWN *wears a small head scarf to cover her thinning hair,*
as she does for most of the play.

ANGELA. I've only been there four and a half months.

DAWN. Well then it won't be too much of an upheaval.

ANGELA. There's still stuff in boxes.

DAWN. Well keep it in boxes. Then it's easier to move again.

ANGELA. Dawn, he's fifteen.

DAWN. He knows where you live.

ANGELA. He's no danger.

DAWN. You don't know that.

ANGELA. Yes I do.

DAWN. Look, I have to play the party line on this one.

ANGELA. He just wants a bit of attention.

DAWN. I'm advising you to move. We can't make you,
obviously, but for safety's sake I have to make a record of
this meeting and the advice I have given.

ANGELA. Whose safety?

DAWN. Yours.

ANGELA. It's nothing to *do* with me. I can't help where he turns up.

Pause.

DAWN. Alright. How do you think he got your address?

ANGELA. I have no idea.

DAWN. It's not on any documents is it?

ANGELA. No.

DAWN. And you've not left anything personal lying around. Have you?

ANGELA. No.

DAWN. Then he must have followed you home one night.

ANGELA. I don't think so.

DAWN. You really should be taking this more seriously, Ange.

ANGELA. He's lonely.

DAWN. Oh come on, you know his case history. He's a violent kid.

ANGELA. Not to me he's not. It's classic attention-seeking. He's lonely. He's rejected. He's virtually illiterate.

Beat.

DAWN. Does he have your phone number?

ANGELA. Only my mobile.

DAWN. The office one.

ANGELA. My personal one.

DAWN. Ange!

ANGELA. What?

DAWN. What is going on with you and this kid? You *know* not to give out that sort of information!

ANGELA. It's for emergencies. He's never used it.

DAWN. Well I'm glad to hear it. Change the number.

ANGELA. There's no need.

DAWN. I'm advising you – officially – to think about moving house and changing your mobile phone.

ANGELA. Well I'll think about it.

DAWN. Good.

Beat.

ANGELA. He only hangs around.

DAWN. I see. And do you talk to him when he 'hangs around'?

ANGELA. He's only done it twice.

DAWN. And last night is three. Do you talk to him?

ANGELA. Sometimes, yeah.

DAWN. Do you let him in?

ANGELA. No!

DAWN. Do you give him anything?

Pause.

Angela. Do you give him anything?

ANGELA. Not really.

DAWN. Oh for Christ's sake. What have you given him? Food? Money? (*Pause.*) Ange. Please don't tell me you've been giving him money.

The door opens. DAMIEN *pops his head round.*

DAMIEN. Dawn – oh, sorry. School's rung in – Adam Leith's absconded again.

DAWN. Speak of the devil. (*To* ANGELA.) He'd better not be you-know-where.

ANGELA. It's alright he'll be round his Mum's, it's their regular day.

DAWN. Not during school hours it's not. Get round there. He's not supposed to see her unsupervised.

ANGELA. I'm there, calm down.

DAWN. *Don't* tell me to calm down.

ANGELA. Fine, stress out.

DAMIEN *starts to go.*

DAWN. Sorry Damien – can you stay a sec?

DAMIEN. 'Course.

ANGELA. Can I go and deal with my client?

DAWN. Yeah – to be continued alright? Paramountcy and partnership Ange – this is about him not you.

ANGELA. Thank you, but I think I've been here long enough to –

DAWN *hands* ANGELA *a legal document.*

DAWN. Children Act 1989 – brush up.

ANGELA. For God's sake Dawn I'm not a / complete fool –

DAWN. You getting a lunch tomorrow?

ANGELA. What? I dunno, tomorrow's miles away.

DAWN. If you do – in here, right? Education want an update on the autistic / kid.

ANGELA. Right.

ANGELA *goes.*

DAWN (*to* DAMIEN). Shut the door.

DAMIEN *does so.*

DAWN (*hushed*). Janine Carlson.

DAMIEN. The home still haven't seen her. She didn't go back last night.

DAWN. What about her Mum's?

DAMIEN. She's never round her Mum's, they hate each other.

DAWN. Right, this is getting serious. Where else are the police checking?

DAMIEN. The police . . . they're not – they haven't – look I thought it best if –

DAWN. Damien – you *have* contacted the police?

Beat.

DAMIEN. It's under control.

DAWN. You haven't have you?

DAMIEN. Dawn, I'm sorry, but if we ring the police in a huge flap *every* time Janine Carlson vanishes for 24 hours, you won't / see her for dust when I turn up to –

DAWN. Damien! She's fifteen! And no-one knows where she is!

DAMIEN. It's wasting police time, this happens every week.

DAWN. She's a minor that's gone missing from our care! / You *have* to report it!

DAMIEN. Dawn, please, I just think the best way forward for Janine is to nurture a trusting relationship where we're not treating / her like –

DAWN. Treating her like what?

DAMIEN. Like a prisoner.

DAWN. We are treating her, Damien, like the vulnerable and confused kid she is, and *you* should be doing your job when / she vanishes and –

DAMIEN. Oh come on, that's not fair – how am I supposed to develop any semblance of trust with the kid when we're having her hauled in by cops / every five minutes?

DAWN. Janine is supposed to be *specialed,* Damien.

DAMIEN. I know this.

DAWN. Right, she's supposed to have one-to-one supervision *24 hours a day* under the terms of her licence –

DAMIEN. Then employ me a care assistant for her –

DAWN. We've *been* through this! I have begged and pleaded with Gordon, because if we have reneged on our commitment to / fund this –

DAMIEN. Which isn't my fault –

DAWN. I'm not saying it is – if she then goes missing under those circumstances – we – that's you and I – are in *deep* trouble. (*Pause.*) If this gets / out –

DAMIEN. It's not going to get out –

DAWN. If anything happens to / her –

DAMIEN. Nothing's going to happen to her. Trust me.

DAWN. Damien – stuff like this, you can't *wing* it.

Pause.

When did Grace last see her?

DAMIEN. Yesterday lunchtime, took her to see her Dad in prison.

DAWN. Well that's just the sort of thing that could send her /
   over the edge –

DAMIEN. What? Janine likes her Dad, that's the highlight of
   the month / seeing him.

DAWN. Get on the phone.

DAMIEN. What?

DAWN. Get on the phone to the police.

DAMIEN. She'll turn up.

DAWN. Get on the phone to the police and report her as
   missing *now.*

   DAWN *holds out a phone.*

DAMIEN. This will jeopardise *all* the progress I've made in
   the last –

DAWN. Do it. And afterwards you can get out there and help
   them look for her.

   DAMIEN *dials sulkily.*

DAMIEN (*into phone*). Yes it's Damien Jackson at Family
   Services, could you put me through to Inspector Colloran in
   Child Protection please? Thank you.

   GORDON *passes.* DAWN *calls after him.*

DAWN. Oh Gordon!

GORDON (*not stopping*). Sorry Dawn, running late. If it's
   important, book in to see me.

DAWN. It's always important!

GORDON. Isn't it just.

   He's gone.

3.

A wrecker's yard.

JANINE under a bonnet fixing a car engine.

*DAMIEN surveys the vehicle. JANINE carries on working
under the bonnet.*

JANINE. Look Damien I know you think you're helping and that, but would you mind just fucking off? If I stay under here he'll just think you're a punter. I can't talk to you, not here. I mean why d'ya have to come here? Hey, you din't ask for us at the gate did ya?

DAMIEN. Ford Falcon, 1982. Three point five litre, sixteen valve, water cooled engine. Like driving a tank. Suspension's a bit shot here though, and those re-treads need changing. These are made in Australia, how the hell did it end up here?

JANINE *comes out from under the bonnet.*

JANINE. You're two years out. It's 1980.

DAMIEN. They didn't re-design the shell til '84 though, did they? I can be forgiven.

JANINE. How d'you know this stuff?

DAMIEN. I had one when I was out there. Get it going on those desert highways and you were away. Cruised like a dream.

JANINE. You drove in the desert?

DAMIEN. Drove everywhere.

JANINE. Where?

DAMIEN. Sydney to Melbourne, Great Ocean Road to Adelaide, Stuart Highway to Alice Springs, saw Ayer's Rock, King's Canyon –

JANINE. Like in that film?

DAMIEN. Priscilla?

JANINE. Nah fuck off. That's that one with all them queers.

DAMIEN. Don't call them / *queers* –

JANINE. Well whatever. Poofs. Not that one.

DAMIEN. Which then?

JANINE. Y'know. Where they drive off the edge at the end.

DAMIEN. Oh, Thelma and Louise.

JANINE. Yeah! I never got that at the end, when they topped themselves. I mean, what d'they do that for?

DAMIEN. Well they were trapped on that cliff –

JANINE. Yeah but they had a gun –

DAMIEN. And they were surrounded by police / and –

JANINE. And so they just should've shot / their way out –

DAMIEN. They were outgunned by about ten to one –

JANINE. So what? In – in – in – oh what the fuck is it – that one where there's all the army at the end and they're surrounded in the shed –

DAMIEN. Butch Cassidy –

JANINE. Yeah! And the Sunshine Kid – and they do it don't they? They go out and fight don't they?

Beat.

DAMIEN. Yeah, they didn't know everyone else was there in that one. They didn't know they were surrounded.

JANINE. Yeah they did, they heard 'em.

DAMIEN. They didn't.

JANINE. They did.

DAMIEN. They didn't.

JANINE. They did!

Beat.

Anyway. It's better than topping yerself like a couple of lezzas.

DAMIEN. Janine you shouldn't call / them –

JANINE. Whatever! Dykes!

Pause.

DAMIEN. You like films.

JANINE. What sort of question is that? Everyone likes films. Better than real life int they?

Beat.

DAMIEN. Hey Janine.

JANINE. What?

DAMIEN. Who'll see me?

JANINE. You what?

DAMIEN. He'll just think I'm a punter, you said. Earlier. Who?

JANINE *retreats under the bonnet.*

JANINE. No-one. You've gotta go now.

DAMIEN. Janine, you know why I'm here.

JANINE. You can't do anything. You're not a copper.

DAMIEN. No, but they're all out looking for you too.

JANINE. Oh *what?*

DAMIEN. Look I'm really sorry, I was *told* to. Forced to, in fact. There's . . . rules we have to follow.

JANINE. Yeah? Well if they turn up here I'm fucking dead. Fucking lot of good rules'll do me then.

DAMIEN. Why? What's going on here?

JANINE. Nothing. I'm just working

DAMIEN. You can't just come and go without letting us know where you are.

JANINE. I'm just working.

DAMIEN. They won't be turning up. I told them *I'd* look here. Save them a job. I knew where you'd be.

JANINE. I'm just *working.*

DAMIEN. You're fifteen Janine. And you're on a licence to be specialed.

JANINE. Well where's my special minder then?

DAMIEN. She's not – there isn't – it's being negotiated.

JANINE. Fuck's sake, what's all the fuss about? Getting me sorted, GCSEs for thickos and all that – what for? Get me a job, innit. Well, I've got a job.

DAMIEN. It's not as simple as that, and you know it. Come on, you're bright, you know how the system works.

JANINE. Fucking system.

DAMIEN. How much does Buddy pay you?

JANINE. Enough.

DAMIEN. Hourly rate? Percentage?

JANINE. Hang on. How do you know about Buddy?

DAMIEN. Everyone knows Buddy. He runs the yard. Doesn't he?

JANINE. I never told you about Buddy.

DAMIEN *holds up the wrecker's yard business card.*

DAMIEN. It's okay. I know you didn't.

JANINE. Just fuck off before he comes over.

DAMIEN. Janine. We have a shared legal responsibility for you.

JANINE. I don't give a shit about all that. You'll get me in trouble.

DAMIEN. What sort of trouble, Janine?

JANINE. Get out of here.

DAMIEN. Trouble like that cut on your cheek?

JANINE. That's from working.

DAMIEN. Or the bruises on your arm?

JANINE. That's oil.

DAMIEN. Does Buddy offer you any other work, Janine?

JANINE *holds out a carburetter.*

JANINE. Take this. Pay for it at the gate. He'll ask otherwise, I don't want him to ask. And try and look normal.

DAMIEN. Janine. I need to know. Is Buddy getting you involved in anything else?

JANINE. Oh fuck off.

DAMIEN. I can't go without you.

JANINE. There'll be trouble. If he sees us – if I leave, he'll – you'll . . . you might get –

DAMIEN. What? I might get hurt?

Beat.

If there's going to be that sort of trouble, I can still call the police.

JANINE. No Damien please – not that, not here. He'd kill me.

DAMIEN. Why? What's the problem with the police?

JANINE. Buddy's just – he just hates 'em!

DAMIEN. Why?

JANINE. 'Cos they're cunts.

Beat.

Look I'm alright here. Just chill out and leave us alone.

DAMIEN. Right. So everything's fine.

JANINE. I said so din't I?

DAMIEN. Where were you last night?

Beat.

Janine. Where were you last night?

Pause.

Okay. How'd it go with your Dad yesterday?

JANINE *shrugs.*

Out soon isn't he?

JANINE. Whoopee.

DAMIEN. Alright. When did you last eat?

JANINE *shrugs.*

Yesterday?

JANINE *shrugs.*

Day before?

JANINE *gets on her back to work on the engine from underneath.*

You can't hide under there.

No answer.

Well look, I'm starving. I'm getting a fry-up in the cafe over the road.

No answer.

You want one? My shout.

No answer.

Janine?

No answer.

Janine come on mate. I've put myself on the line here. I should've reported you missing last night, but I trusted that you'd be able to look after yourself.

Pause.

I trusted that you'd get in touch.

Pause.

Mmm. I can smell those sausages from here. I'll see you in there, yeah?

JANINE. Go to the gate. Buy the carburetter. And go.

DAMIEN. I'll see you in five, yeah?

No answer.

I'll see you in there.

JANINE. Yeah. Whatever.

4.

Fifth-floor walkway outside the front door of a council flat.

ADAM *wears a scruffy school uniform. He stands at the front door with one hand holding the buzzer down constantly. With the other he smokes a spliff.*

ANGELA *enters, out of breath.*

ANGELA. Sorry. Got held up. You okay?

ADAM *shrugs.*

No answer?

ADAM. Yeah. No answer.

ANGELA. Really? Oh.

ADAM. Been trying since half two.

ANGELA. Oh no. She definitely said four?

ADAM. Yeah. S'always four.

ANGELA. Four o'clock today?

ADAM. Yeah. Tuesdays at four.

ANGELA. Look stop that, stop it. She'll have heard you if she's in.

ADAM. She said four.

ANGELA. It is four. She knew you were coming. Maybe something's come up.

ADAM. Who cares? She doesn't.

ANGELA. Of course she does, she's your Mum. Adam, stop ringing the bell.

ADAM *stops ringing and leans over the edge of the walkway.*

ADAM. We gonna wait?

ANGELA. This really isn't on, this is your contact time. I'm sorry, of course we'll wait.

ADAM *spits over the edge.*

Please don't do that.

Pause.

How was school?

ADAM (*shrugs*). Same.

Pause.

I could jump off here.

ANGELA. Don't be silly.

Beat.

ADAM. Angie, I've cut my hand.

ANGELA. Where.

ADAM. Look.

ANGELA. Ooh looks nasty. How did you do that?

ADAM. Cat did it.

ANGELA. Whose cat?

ADAM. Dunno.

ANGELA. Should get some antiseptic on it.

ADAM. S'alright, doesn't hurt. Look.

ADAM *scratches at the wound.*

ANGELA. Stop that, you'll make it worse. What's the point of doing that?

ADAM *shrugs. Pause.*

Did you have art today?

ADAM. Yeah.

ANGELA. How's that painting going? The coursework.

ADAM. It's not.

ANGELA. Oh. The Holocaust one? I liked that. Have you started another instead?

ADAM. Nah. Took that one down the field at lunch and pissed on it.

ANGELA. What?

ADAM. Pissed all down it. Colours all ran off, it was well funny.

ANGELA. Adam, that was your coursework for the year.

ADAM. So what? It was shit.

ANGELA. It was good.

ADAM. Might hand it in then. Stinks now.

ANGELA. Adam you're good at art, we've discussed this, you've got a natural talent.

ADAM. Bollocks have I.

ANGELA. You have. Mr. Morrison agrees.

ADAM. He hates me.

ANGELA. He thinks a lot of you, he's told me. How are you gonna pass if you do silly things like damaging your work?

ADAM *shrugs. Pause.*

ADAM. You haven't told us off yet.

ANGELA. What for?

ADAM. Smoking gange.

ANGELA. Adam, I don't *care* if you smoke gange. It's the least of your worries to be frank.

ADAM. So I'm allowed?

ANGELA. No, I'm just not going to notice. Especially not if it calms you down.

Pause.

ADAM. I ate a mushroom.

ANGELA. I'm sorry?

ADAM. Down here on the floor, where all the water runs, there's little mushrooms growing. Look.

ANGELA. Adam, that's a gutter! What are you playing at?

ADAM. Thought it might be magic.

ANGELA. Oh God, there's a dead cat down here! Tell me you're having me on.

ADAM. Dead cat? Let's have a look.

ANGELA. Leave it alone, it'll be filthy.

ADAM. Oh no.

ANGELA. What is it?

ADAM. That's Mum's cat.

ANGELA. You're kidding.

ADAM. No, it's Sammy. He was her only friend.

ANGELA. Adam, did you really eat a mushroom from the gutter?

ADAM. Mum'll be well upset.

ANGELA. She'll be more upset if you've poisoned yourself.

ADAM. Look, someone's killed it. There's blood.

ANGELA. Get away from it.

ADAM (*toying with the spliff*). I could burn its eyes out.

ANGELA. Don't be disgusting. Come on, we're going.

ADAM. Could stuff it through Mum's letterbox.

ANGELA. Don't be so stupid.

ADAM. That'd teach her.

ANGELA. Adam . . . you didn't –

    ADAM *picks it up.*

    No don't touch it!

ADAM. S'alright, it's only a cat.

ANGELA. Leave it, it'll be covered in diseases. Put it down!

ADAM. Ah, it's still warm. If only she'd been here, she could've looked after it.

ANGELA. Adam! Put it down and come with me!

ADAM *throws the cat over the edge of the wall.*

Adam for God's sake! There could be people down there!

ADAM. That'd be funny.

ANGELA. Adam – you are fifteen years old. Will you stop behaving like you're five.

ADAM. Fuck off.

ANGELA. Come on, I'm taking you to Casualty.

ADAM. What?

ANGELA. You're covered in filth and you've eaten poison. Come on.

ADAM. Aren't we gonna wait for Mum?

ANGELA. Not now you've done this, no.

ADAM. I didn't really eat a mushroom.

ANGELA. Well we've still got to get you cleaned up. There's a tap downstairs. Come on.

They go.

5.

A bar in Covent Garden.

GRACE *and* ADELE. ADELE *flicking through holiday snaps. She gasps at one in particular and holds it to her chest.*

ADELE. God I forgot to tell you! You'll never *guess* who was there on the beach!

GRACE. Who?

ADELE. Guess.

GRACE. I can't.

ADELE. Right next to us, perched on a towel. Think school.

GRACE. Oh I don't know.

ADELE *squints through one eye.*

What are you doing?

ADELE. Think eyeballs. I could've *died.*

GRACE. Del, I'm tired.

ADELE *holds out the photo.*

ADELE. Janet Engelmann.

GRACE. Who?

ADELE. Glassy! With the *glass eye.* (*Indicating photo.*) There.

GRACE. Oh.

ADELE. She's still got it right, you can't really see there – but it's a better one now, you'd hardly guess – but she was *there* with *him.*

ADELE *holds out another photo.*

GRACE. Oh right. Who's that?

ADELE. Just the *fittest* model-type diving instructor you've *ever* seen.

GRACE. Oh right.

ADELE. Apart from he's only got one leg! See?

GRACE. Oh yeah.

ADELE. It was brilliant! Me and Tony *pissed* ourselves.

GRACE. Pretty funny.

ADELE. But you know what?

GRACE. What?

ADELE. She was *really* nice.

GRACE. No way.

ADELE. Yeah! We got chatting – and get this right – she started her own *prosthetics* company after school. Seriously. Legs and arms and all that. And with all that new money in the NHS and them having to tender out, she's making a *mint.*

GRACE. Yeah?

ADELE. Yeah! Glassy. Of all people. There in the Azores.

Beat.

GRACE. I met a two-year-old girl today. Hospital visit. In for some knock or scrape on her leg. And the doctor's seen these other cuts. Further up. And they go right up. He said they could only have been caused by broken glass.

Pause.

ADELE. Oh.

GRACE. I'm sorry to put that picture in your head but it's been on my mind.

Pause. ADELE *puts the photos down.*

ADELE. How . . . how do you do it?

GRACE. We're prosecuting. He'll get ten years.

ADELE. No I mean . . . *you.* How do *you* cope?

GRACE. Me? Fuck's sake Del, I'm the lucky one.

Beat.

ADELE. I . . . I admire you.

GRACE. Don't be patronising.

ADELE. Gracie, I'm not, I'm really not. I just . . . I just don't understand. I can't get my head round why you'd wanna –

GRACE. I'll tell you why Adele. Because no other fucker gives a shit that's why.

ADELE. Hey calm down, I'm not getting at you.

GRACE. And because this stuff – it's going on about two hundred yards in that direction – (GRACE *points.*) – and no-one seems to care. Our lot, us trendy trendy fuckers in here, how many of us give a shit?

ADELE. Look what it's doing to you already.

GRACE. What?

ADELE. Look at you. On edge. You're never like this.

GRACE. Why is it 'on edge' to be passionate about my work?

ADELE. It's not, I'm not saying that.

GRACE. Why is it 'on edge' to care about the people around us?

ADELE. You're going off on one, I'm not saying any of that.

GRACE. You're in 'media' sales.

ADELE. So?

GRACE. So what would you care?

ADELE. Jesus Christ.

GRACE. You and Tony have holidays in The Azores.

ADELE. Don't take the moral high ground with me.

Pause.

I couldn't do what you do that's all.

Pause.

Anyway. She said to say hello.

GRACE. Who?

ADELE. Glassy. Janet.

GRACE. Right.

Pause. ADELE *offers cigarettes.*

ADELE. Fag?

GRACE. No.

Beat.

Yeah. Yeah cheers.

She takes one.

6.

Team meeting in the large office.

DAWN, SHIRLEY, ANGELA, DAMIEN *and* GRACE.

DAWN *rifles through papers and files.* DAMIEN *plays with a large radio-controlled Monster Truck.* GRACE *with notepad prepares to take minutes.*

The opening dialogues between ANGELA *and* SHIRLEY / GRACE *and* DAMIEN *run concurrently.* GRACE *and* DAMIEN*'s conversation is the more audible.*

ANGELA. There's important lessons in there, it's textbook stuff.

SHIRLEY. It is not a textbook, it is Denise's life.

ANGELA. I'll mention it hypothetically.

SHIRLEY. You'll do nothing of the sort, Angela.

ANGELA. Why are you being so defensive?

SHIRLEY. Why are you so damn keen to interfere?

ANGELA. All I'm saying is –

GRACE (*to* DAMIEN, *of the car*). Oh my God! I've not seen one for years.

DAMIEN. Oh, they're *so* much better now. Look, five gears and there's like a – a *radar* thing on the handset.

GRACE. Wicked. Is it yours?

DAMIEN. No it's for Charlie, my boy. He's two this week.

GRACE. Ah, bless. Two, though? Isn't he a bit young for it?

DAMIEN. They grow into these things.

DAWN (*to* ANGELA *and* SHIRLEY). Right – stop bickering please you two. (*To* DAMIEN.) Damien, put it away it's not playschool. (*To* GRACE.) Grace, try Gordon's extension one last time would you, there's a love.

GRACE. Sure.

GRACE *dials a number.*

DAWN. Right. I'm seeing Mandy at half past so this can't drag on.

DAMIEN. Mandy Owens? I thought she'd gone back to Huddersfield.

SHIRLEY. She was a sweet girl.

DAWN. She's dropped out of college.

SHIRLEY. Silly child.

GRACE. Still no answer.

DAWN. Honestly. Ange, you don't know where Gordon is do you? He seems to keep you informed better than most.

ANGELA. He was meeting councillors or something this morning. I don't really know.

DAWN. Well we can't wait any longer so we'll make a start and he'll just have to catch up. Now. You'll all have heard about Shirley's casualty upstairs yesterday – how's she getting on Shirl?

SHIRLEY. Denise is okay, she had a stomach pump for internal bleeding but no haemorrhaging. She's in for observation, so tomorrow will have to be postponed. But the Emergency Protection Order's running out so it'll have to be / Thursday at the latest.

ANGELA. Was it that boyfriend?

SHIRLEY. Most probably.

ANGELA. Bastard.

SHIRLEY. Terry's an old one of mine.

ANGELA. He'll have her too scared to press charges.

SHIRLEY. I've seen it a hundred times, she is just frightened about the child.

DAMIEN. We taking those burns on the kid as deliberately inflicted now?

DAWN. Look, none of us have got time to go into the ins and outs of the case – we'll have the usual strategy meeting with the police and proceed from there. The point is that you should all be aware that the silent panic alarm in that room is there for these situations too –

GRACE. Sorry – am I minuting this?

DAWN. Yes. And if the foyer needs clearing during incidents like that –

ANGELA. Yeah. Look, Dawn –

DAWN. Yuh.

ANGELA. I just wanted to bring this up quickly, and – well – I thought it might be particularly valuable for our trainee –

SHIRLEY. Angela, this is a discussion I didn't really want to get into –

ANGELA. No I think it's important because Shirley was telling me that Denise has asked for a white social worker for her case.

SHIRLEY. For goodness' sake Angela.

ANGELA. She suddenly says she doesn't want Shirley any more, after a year of working together. I just thought it might be helpful to air this and just sort of, well, unpack the issues involved really –

DAMIEN. 'Unpack'? You sound like Gordon.

DAWN. Where *is* he?

An office phone rings. GRACE *moves.*

Ignore it please, downstairs can take it.

SHIRLEY. It might be Gordon.

DAWN. Okay, answer it please.

GRACE *answers it.*

GRACE (*into phone*). Hello, Family Support Team?

GRACE *brief phone call impro.*

ANGELA. Anyway look – Denise's request to Shirley is a recognised symptom of internalised oppression.

SHIRLEY. I'm sorry?

ANGELA. Oppression. Your clients've internalised white culture so much that they're oppressing their own colour. They see white workers as being more powerful than black. They think a white keyworker will get results for them 'cos they've got more authority – I've seen it before.

SHIRLEY. Oh *have* you now?

GRACE *hangs up.*

GRACE. Wasn't Gordon.

DAWN (*mutters*). Goodness' sake.

SHIRLEY. I don't think so. I just know Terence too well. He'll have bullied her into asking because he knows he'll be found out.

DAWN. It's a tricky one –

GRACE. Sorry, am I minuting this too?

SHIRLEY. No.

ANGELA. Yes.

DAWN. But we don't really have time to –

SHIRLEY. Dawn, if you look at your sheet I have booked in to see you to discuss it next week –

GRACE. We're doing this at college! Isn't it that they're worried about stuff creeping out, that someone from their own community will leak information?

SHIRLEY. I'm nothing to do with their community – I'm Dominican and they're Jamaican.

ANGELA. No, it's self-oppression, it's more and more common.

SHIRLEY. So am *I* oppressed Angela?

ANGELA. Of course you are. Less so because you're an educated professional but –

DAWN. Can we move on please?

GRACE. I think it might be secrets.

ANGELA. What?

DAWN. Grace, please –

DAMIEN. Grace –

GRACE. You know – there's something going on, and – and they think they can keep it from a white worker more easily.

DAMIEN*'s radio-controlled truck whirs into life and moves across the floor.*

ANGELA. How?

DAWN. Damien don't do that.

GRACE. Over-sensitivity. They think we're too PC.

ANGELA. Rubbish.

DAWN. I'm really sorry people, but I'm gonna have to rein this in – there just isn't time. I've got that lunch meeting in . . . (*She checks her watch.*) . . . five minutes ago.

ANGELA. Hang on, this family should have their dissent recorded.

SHIRLEY. It is not dissent, it is a request.

ANGELA. It's vocalising their oppression. It's a cry for help.

DAWN. Well whatever, it'll be recorded – note it on their file Shirl, but we just don't have the resources to give everyone a choice. Now. The other thing last week was Grace's little mishap, which I accept full responsibility for in misjudging the case.

GRACE. I'm fine.

ANGELA. You're not fine, you were attacked.

DAWN. She's fine. But again, measures are now in place to protect you all in these eventualities. This –

DAWN *holds up a thing like a mobile phone which quietly beeps*

– is a Global Positioning System handset, GPS for short.

SHIRLEY. A what?

DAMIEN. Like a radar.

ANGELA. What is this – Star Trek?

DAWN. It simply gives a signal back to a central computer that can tell us your exact location in the city.

ANGELA. What's the point of that?

SHIRLEY. New-fangled nonsense.

DAMIEN. I think they're cool.

DAWN. It's optional to carry it at the moment but on some cases the department will insist –

ANGELA. Sorry, but wouldn't a rape alarm be more useful?

DAMIEN*'s radio-controlled truck moves across the floor again.*

DAWN. You can get one of those at cost through Human Resources at the Council.

ANGELA. Christ's sake.

DAWN. Damien stop that please.

DAMIEN. Sorry.

DAWN. Anyway it's not my idea, it's come down from on high. Anyway, there it is. Shirley I'm giving it to you for that trip to –

SHIRLEY. Nonsense. I don't need a silly thing like that.

DAWN. Well, it's optional. But I should point out to the new recruits amongst us that the chances of getting attacked are very very slight. And nothing at all compared to nursing. Or Benefits Agency.

ANGELA. How reassuring.

SHIRLEY. This is silly.

DAWN. What's that Shirley?

SHIRLEY. This – this *fear* of the public, the *fear* of forming relationships, it's nonsense. Relationships are what we do! He was scared of her taking the boy away, he wasn't going to / hurt her.

DAWN. Well in our new litigation culture we can't take that risk / any more.

ANGELA. Well Grace isn't going to sue us. Are you?

DAMIEN. Ange, to be fair the guy did have a knife.

GRACE. It was fine, I'm fine.

ANGELA. It was Jason Lawley's dad wasn't it?

Another phone rings. GRACE *answers it. Her conversation with* DAWN *and the telephone carries on whilst* DAMIEN *and* ANGELA*'s conversation runs over the top.*

GRACE. Hello, Family Support?

DAWN (*to* GRACE). Is it Gordon?

GRACE (*into phone*). Sorry, is this Gordon? It isn't?

DAWN (*to* GRACE). Hang up.

GRACE (*into phone*). Sorry, could you call back a bit later? Okay, thanks – sorry.

DAMIEN. Yeah, and I *know* he's / paralysed from the waist down –

ANGELA. Paralysed from the waist down – so what bloody harm was he going to do / crawling round on his belly –

DAMIEN. The guy has a paranoid military fantasy –

DAWN. Look! The point is we've all learned from the experience haven't we?

ANGELA. Have we?

DAWN. Yes. Now –

ANGELA. Well if you will send in the untrained with all guns blazing –

GRACE (*defiant*). I didn't do that.

Beat. GRACE *and* ANGELA *minor stand-off.*

DAWN. Now listen, it's at times like this –

DAMIEN. It's alright, it was my fault. I should have come with you Grace. Overworked, stretched too thin – blah blah. You've heard it all before I'm sure. Anyway, I'm sorry.

GRACE. Thank you.

DAWN. Okay. Good. Now –

ANGELA (*muttering*). If we got the bloody funding we asked for . . .

DAWN. I'm sorry Angela?

ANGELA. If we got the funds and the staff we need then *trainees* wouldn't be doing dangerous house calls in the / first place would they?

DAWN. Alright! You all know we're awaiting a decision on this year's bid to the Council. I'm meeting with Gordon about it later this week. I can't tell you any more till then.

DAMIEN*'s truck moves again.*

Damien I will *confiscate* that thing.

DAMIEN. I just leant on the stick by mistake, I'm sorry.

Another phone rings. No-one answers it.

DAWN. Now I'm sorry people, but I've *got* to shoot. Ange – do you wanna take over for your item?

ANGELA. Sure.

DAMIEN (*to* GRACE, *of the minutes*). It's alright, you can skip this bit.

ANGELA. No you can't.

SHIRLEY. Oh, and my retirement do next week, people –

DAWN. Oh yeah –

SHIRLEY. Barbecue at mine next Thursday, all welcome.

DAWN. Diaries everyone, Shirley's done – what is it – thirty years?

SHIRLEY. Well, twenty-eight.

DAWN. Twenty-eight – so she deserves a good send off, yeah?

DAMIEN. / Sure.

GRACE. / Wicked.

ANGELA. She deserves a bloody medal.

DAWN. Yeah, right. (*To* ANGELA.) Okay. All yours. See ya.

DAWN *goes*.

ANGELA (*to group*). Right. Well it's about the flag on the roof. I think we should think about taking it down during the Football Championships –

DAMIEN. Oh God, I really don't have time for this. Grace – stop minuting, you / don't need to.

ANGELA. No actually, I think we need to talk about this!

Another phone rings.

GRACE. Shall I get that?

ANGELA. / No.

DAMIEN. Yes.

GRACE (*into phone*). Hello Family Support?

GRACE *brief phone call impro.*

SHIRLEY. What's the matter with the flag?

ANGELA. The St. George flag has become associated with *racism* and extremist attitudes –

DAMIEN. Come on Gracie, I'll get you lunch.

ANGELA. Damien! Sport is symbolic – she needs an awareness of these things!

DAMIEN. Fancy a Big Mac, Gracie?

ANGELA. It's about putting a sensitive image across to the clients – I mean what do we want them to think?

DAMIEN. I want them to think we're spending our time on stuff that'll make a difference to *them*, not *us*.

ANGELA. Damien!

GRACE (*into phone*). Just a sec. (*To* ANGELA.) Sorry – (*To* DAMIEN.) It's the police, they want a strategy meeting about Janine – maybe put an appeal out on the local news?

DAMIEN (*to* GRACE). Alright come on – hope you've brought sarnies. (*To* ANGELA.) Sorry Ange.

ANGELA. Oh don't mind me.

GRACE (*into phone*). Okay, half two. Cheers, see ya.

GRACE *hangs up.* DAMIEN *and* GRACE *gather their things,* DAMIEN *picks up the truck.*

Several phones ring simultaneously.

GRACE (*to* DAMIEN, *of the truck*). We're taking that down the police station are we?

DAMIEN. Right, no. You're right.

DAMIEN *puts it down.*

SHIRLEY. I'm sorry Angela, I have to get going too.

ANGELA. We're a multi-cultural society! There is no Britain any more – Shirley, what if you want to – want to support *Jamaica* during the World Cup, then you've got every right to –

SHIRLEY. I don't have no time for football.

Another phone rings. SHIRLEY *starts to go.*

ANGELA. Christ's sake, don't we have time to *think* any more?

GORDON *enters with two Starbucks coffees.*

SHIRLEY/DAMIEN/GRACE. Hello Gordon / Hi there / Hiya.

GORDON. Sorry everyone – got held up.

ANGELA *answers a phone.*

ANGELA (*into phone*). What!

GORDON. Oh blast, have I missed all the fun?

GORDON *hands* ANGELA *one of the coffees. She winks at him.*

Now then. Team meeting.

7.

Busy coffee bar, lunchtime.

DAWN *with* MANDY, *light lunch.*

DAWN. Travel and tourism? Mykonos resort? Sun sea sex? What happened to all that?

MANDY. Didn't find it in Huddersfield.

DAWN. Oh Mand. So where now?

MANDY. Dunno. Got a flat.

DAWN. Have you? Well that's good. That's great.

MANDY. Deptford way.

DAWN. Oh you haven't gone far then, that's my old patch.

MANDY. It's a nice place. Better than that shite you sorted me out with way back when.

DAWN. Hey, I did my best for you kiddo.

MANDY. I'm kidding ya Dawn, I wouldn't be here if I din't like ya would I? If I weren't *grateful* and that.

DAWN. I suppose. How're your flatmates? Can they get you any work?

MANDY. Maybe. There's only one, the one guy. It's his place.

DAWN. Oh right. But you're not . . . you know.

MANDY. Am I fuck. In his dreams.

DAWN *laughs.*

But yeah, Brad's one of those people what *knows* people and where people know him. Ya know what I mean?

DAWN. Right.

MANDY. So he might be able to sort us out, just for the time being like.

DAWN. What . . . what sort of thing?

MANDY. Oh you know, this and that.

DAWN. Mand. Brad who?

MANDY. I dunno. Bradley.

DAWN. Bradley who?

MANDY. Oh I dunno.

DAWN. How long you been there?

MANDY. Oh I dunno.

DAWN. You don't know how long you've been living there?

MANDY. Oh, couple of months.

DAWN. It's Bradley Carlson isn't it?

MANDY. Who? I dunno.

DAWN. Well I do. Janine's brother.

MANDY. Who?

DAWN. Mandy! You know as well as I do – he's a – I can't believe you're – oh you silly cow.

MANDY. What? Fuck off.

DAWN. Bradley Carlson was one of mine – his little sister's one of ours now. Mandy don't pretend you don't know that family – that boy's a gangster.

MANDY. What Brad? No he ain't, he's lovely.

DAWN. Amanda – if you've knowingly moved into a flat with Bradley Carlson you will *seriously* go down in my estimation.

MANDY. In your what?

DAWN. Oh, Mandy.

Beat.

MANDY. Look, Dawn.

DAWN. What?

MANDY. I've been meaning to ask ya –

DAWN. Yeah I think I know what's coming –

MANDY. Well things are difficult!

DAWN. Well you won't make it easy for yourself will ya?

MANDY. Well you try living on fifty quid a week!

DAWN. I have! We've got more in common than you think kiddo.

MANDY. Well help us out then!

DAWN. Mand – you've left care. We helped you as much as we could – over and above what we had to in fact. You're a big girl now.

MANDY. Just to tide us over, like you've helped us before –

DAWN. Yeah when you were my responsibility.

MANDY. You're a manager now.

DAWN. So what?

MANDY. You're the boss.

DAWN. I'm certainly not that.

MANDY. You can authorise stuff like that.

DAWN. I certainly can't.

MANDY. Just this week, just for the rent.

DAWN. The rent.

MANDY. Yeah.

DAWN. You want me to authorise cash payments from an –

MANDY. Yeah.

DAWN. From an *audited* departmental budget –

MANDY. Yeah.

DAWN. For you to give directly to an ex-client and known violent criminal.

MANDY. Yeah.

DAWN. Well then you're far from the worldly and streetwise kid I thought you were, Mandy.

Pause.

Okay. How have you been paying the rent up to now?

MANDY. What?

DAWN. You heard.

MANDY. I've just – I've been – sometimes Brad . . .

DAWN. What?

MANDY. I've managed okay? I've managed.

DAWN. Well we both know what that means don't we?

MANDY. Right, fuck off.

MANDY *stands.*

DAWN. Mand –

MANDY. No, fuck right off – I'm not a fuckin whore you bald bitch. I shouldn't have come should I? I should've known better than to ask for help off one of your lot, you're no better than the fuckin pigs.

DAWN. Sit down!

MANDY *flinches.*

Sit. Down.

MANDY *sits slowly.*

This is difficult for me too. We – I – once had a duty of care for you. Now. That shared parental responsibility has expired. But sometimes it's not as simple as that. Of *course* I want to look out for you. Of *course* I want to make sure you're okay. I mean, what's the point of all that time and effort if we send you out there just to crash and burn? I like you Mandy. I like you a lot. I had a little girl like you once. There's a lot of things you don't tell your clients, a lot of things. I sometimes thought we were peas in a pod, you and I. But I will *not* compromise myself to keep you in squalid and dangerous conditions.

Pause.

MANDY. I didn't know you had a daughter.

DAWN. We're not in touch.

MANDY. So help *me.*

DAWN. The thing is . . . The sad thing is Mand, if you were a year younger I could have. Easy. The government's . . . there's a new law come out about what we do with kids in your situation.

MANDY. I'm not a kid.

DAWN. Well exactly – Care Leavers. The Care Leaver's Act. It's just coming into effect. We now have a duty to look after you from eighteen to twenty-four years old.

MANDY. Shit.

DAWN. Now look. That doesn't mean –

MANDY. Yeah it does – twenty-five, let us sink. That's what it means.

DAWN. No. Look, I could *see* – I'm not promising but I could *see* about getting you some food vouchers –

MANDY. Food vouchers?

DAWN. For a limited period –

MANDY. Fuckin food vouchers?

DAWN. Mandy I'm sorry. If there's no Court Order in place and you're beyond the age of –

MANDY. I'm screwing that cunt for my rent and fuckin *food* vouchers?

Pause.

I suppose I've slipped the net. Haven't I?

DAWN. Mandy. Your case is closed.

8.

Restaurant, evening.

GORDON *and* ANGELA *finishing a meal. Both dressed up.* GORDON *is drunk.*

GORDON. And she turned up on one of those TV makeover documentaries.

ANGELA. Never.

GORDON. I swear. 'Divorced Divas' or something. Followed her through Chelsea with Carol Smilie, kitted her out in all these boutiques. Then secretly filmed her on the date.

ANGELA. Oh my God. Did you tell her you'd seen it?

GORDON. No. We've not spoken for a couple of years.

ANGELA. Oh how funny. How did she get on?

GORDON. I can't remember.

ANGELA. Oh I'm sorry. You poor thing, it must have been horrible.

GORDON. I didn't watch it all.

ANGELA. No. I can imagine.

Beat.

I can't help noticing you still wear the ring.

ANGELA *indicates his wedding ring.*

GORDON. Actually, do you know what? I can't get it off.

ANGELA. Really?

GORDON. Honestly. Look.

> GORDON *tugs at it gently.*

ANGELA. Must've put on weight. Can I have a go?

> GORDON *retracts his hand.*

GORDON. Actually I was yanking at it before I came out. It's gone a bit red.

ANGELA. Oh poor you. Have you tried butter?

GORDON. What?

ANGELA. Butter. It helps ease it off.

GORDON. Oh right.

ANGELA. Here.

> ANGELA *holds out a pack of butter from a pot on the table. Pause. Then he takes it from her.*

GORDON. I'll have a crack at it later.

ANGELA. Right.

GORDON. Right.

> GORDON *puts the butter in his jacket pocket.*

ANGELA. How did Simon cope?

GORDON. Oh, he can take whatever's thrown at him.

ANGELA. Can he?

GORDON. Yuh. Studying Genetics. I mean, bloody hell.

ANGELA. Bright kid. Like father like son?

> GORDON *drains his glass.*

GORDON. Simon's gay.

ANGELA. Oh.

GORDON. It's fine. The psychological perspective is that he felt betrayed by his mother so doesn't trust women. What do you think?

ANGELA. Um. I don't think we can help who we are.

GORDON. Oh is that right?

ANGELA. Not when it comes to sexuality. Genetics'll tell you that.

GORDON. Right. So does the same rule apply across the board?

ANGELA. How do you mean?

GORDON. Well take me. From age twelve I've always had a job. After my mother left, my father developed MS and we needed another income. University was out of the question and I've worked ever since. What does that make me?

ANGELA. Um. Well. It indicates a strong mind. An ability to pull through.

GORDON. Right. So we all have certain tendencies that are predetermined.

ANGELA. Tendencies, yes.

GORDON *fills his wine glass.*

GORDON. Alcoholism, for example.

ANGELA. You're not an alcoholic.

Beat.

Are you?

GORDON. Not often.

Smiles. Indicates bottle.

Help yourself. Cheers.

ANGELA. *Tendencies* are pre-determined, Gordon. *Certainties* aren't at all.

GORDON. You know I was thinking about this the other day.

ANGELA. Uh-huh.

GORDON. Yes, I have a bit of time to do that these days. And it occurred to me that the determinist argument is all bollocks.

ANGELA. Okay. So –

GORDON. Because you see it does seem to exclude the possibility that I might have got where I am because I helped *myself.*

ANGELA. Well I'm sure that's true but –

GORDON. An ability to work one's arse off isn't pre-determined. Anyone can do it.

ANGELA. Well there *are* mitigating factors / which mean that people can't always –

GORDON. I'd like to be able to believe that Angela, really I would. Because you see it'd make our job make sense wouldn't it?

ANGELA. Right. In what way exactly?

GORDON. Well wouldn't it be *lovely* if we were just there as a warm and fluffy safety net – hm? – a cushion against unavoidable suffering. Like a – like a *vet.* But we're not are we?

ANGELA. We're not vets, no.

GORDON. No. And the difference is that we spend most of our time dealing with ordinary people's infuriating fuck ups. Don't we?

ANGELA. Yes, the unavoidable fuck ups of the deprived and the uneducated. I'm sorry you find them infuriating.

GORDON. Well I get by because I'm an optimist.

ANGELA. Are you?

GORDON. Damn right. I believe people can change. Make mature choices. I *choose* to drink. And I allow myself that pleasure because I'm mature enough to cope with the hang-over. Same with parenting. I put off having Simon until I'd topped twenty-five grand. It's a question of responsibility.

ANGELA. And what about our responsibility to the child of an alcoholic?

Pause.

GORDON. All I'm asking / is –

ANGELA. I know what you're asking.

GORDON. – is do you ever wonder to yourself just what the hell we think we're doing?

ANGELA. No. I don't.

GORDON. Oh come on. Look at all these resources getting pumped into this never-ending *service* – yes? – well, do you never stop to wonder why such an *expensive* service / exists –

ANGELA. The expense / of it isn't –

GORDON. – to support such a tiny amount of people –

ANGELA. Right well the thing is –

GORDON. – such a tiny amount of people who really are largely in such a state –

ANGELA. Yes –

GORDON. – in such a *state* largely through their own *fault*?

Pause.

I wonder that quite a lot.

ANGELA. I see.

GORDON. Good.

ANGELA. Gordon, surely being on the right side of this argument is a pre-requisite to doing your job?

GORDON. It's my job, Angela, to consider these questions. To inform the compromises I'm forever being asked to make.

ANGELA. Gordon, how can it be a child's fault that they've been sexually abused?

GORDON. No look, please don't misunderstand me. I'm not questioning the value of the work –

ANGELA. I should hope not.

GORDON. – it's fantastic what you all do on the front line – I mean, beyond me, all that, just beyond me.

ANGELA. I'm sure it is.

GORDON. I managed a private care home once, God that was quite enough for me. All that shouting. So I suppose I'm just sort of unpacking it, really. Unpacking the issues. Philosophically.

Beat.

ANGELA. I see. You like that term.

GORDON. Yes. It interests me to do that.

ANGELA. Yes. Unpack.

GORDON. Yes.

ANGELA. Philosophically.

GORDON. Yes.

Pause.

I mean, when people have *clearly* – as they often have – have *clearly* had a – a – a less than ideal start in life, if you then give them their – their *lodgings,* some – some *income,* access to this specialist advice, the 'one stop shops' – all these *free services* – and they *still* fail to take responsibility, to take up their place in society . . . what then?

ANGELA. You keep trying.

GORDON. Yes, but why?

ANGELA. Because, Gordon, this section of society that we don't really like to think about too much – these people have a disproportionately large presence in the crime figures, in the school drop-out rates, in the dole queue. Christ, I don't have to tell you all this.

GORDON. Yes look, I know the arguments –

ANGELA. They go on to become drug addicts, NHS patients, drunk drivers – or – or – prison inmates – the crap parents of / tomorrow – soaking up your taxes in hospital costs and crown prosecutions. It's *preventive.*

GORDON. Yes yes yes no yes, I understand all this, *listen –* I accept it, but what I'm *wondering* is . . . well. If you look at the enormous cost of this 'preventive' service, compared to the similarly large cost of policing the streets and running rehab programmes or whatever if our profession, let's say, wasn't *there* . . . is it really saving us all that much? As a society?

Pause.

ANGELA. That's not a philosophical question, it's an economic one.

GORDON. Well –

ANGELA. Philosophically, Gordon, I think you've missed the point.

GORDON. No, Angela, please – I'm not *attacking* anything.

ANGELA. And I'm not defending anything.

GORDON. Right.

ANGELA. Right. I know it's flawed.

GORDON. Well exactly. If Gloria ran *her* business the way we run *our* business . . . well, she'd be *out* of business.

ANGELA. It's not a business. In fact, it's the complete *opposite* / of business.

GORDON. Damn right – it's one long *compromise* and nothing ever gets done.

ANGELA. Tell me about it.

GORDON. 'Working in *partnership*'. 'Co-operating as *partners*'. Like some wet gay couple.

ANGELA. I think you've had too much to drink.

GORDON. Businesses do not *compromise*. We could learn a thing or two.

ANGELA. Hah! Do you know what I did before I did this?

GORDON. What's that?

ANGELA. I worked in the City. Gold and silver bullion transfers across markets. I know how businesses work. Why d'you think I left?

GORDON. I never knew that. How interesting. A disillusioned executive.

ANGELA. It was a long time ago.

GORDON. Then you of *all* people should know – if Social Services were floated, if it were a service for sale, no-one would buy it.

Beat.

ANGELA. You've never actually worked at the coal face in this profession have you?

GORDON. I trained in *managing*, Angela. People – things – money. That's what I do. I *manage*.

Beat.

ANGELA. Maybe you need to get out. I think maybe you're having . . . some sort of . . .

GORDON. What? What am I having Angela? You tell me, hm? Unleash that famous opinion.

ANGELA. I think you might be having some sort of mid-life crisis.

GORDON. Oh really? The problem lies with me does it? It's inconceivable that there might be anything amiss in this heaving smorgasbord of bureaucracy? This – this – poisoned feast we're force-feeding to the lazy and the weak and the mad. Oh no, it's all thundering along nicely. It's just one man's mid-life crisis, getting in the way.

ANGELA. Gordon. Get a new job.

GORDON. Oh I am.

ANGELA. Good. You're helping no-one here.

GORDON. I've applied for Area Director.

ANGELA. Oh good God.

GORDON. Gloria left me with Simon. Pranced off with Carol Smilie. I have to be here. This is what I'm qualified to do.

ANGELA. I think I'd like to get the bill now please.

GORDON. At my level you're a diplomat. Nothing more.

ANGELA. I'd like to go.

GORDON. A hod-carrier for directives.

ANGELA. I'm sorry, this was a mistake and I'd like to go now, please.

GORDON. My life's been one long compromise, did you know that?

ANGELA. Gordon –

GORDON. Well I won't do it any more. I refuse.

ANGELA. Christ, where's the fucking waiter?

GORDON. Do you believe some people are worth more than others?

ANGELA. Would you shut up?

GORDON. Do you? I do. I don't know why we treat everyone the same, I don't know why we bother, the ungrateful little shits.

ANGELA *takes hold of her glass.*

ANGELA. If you don't shut up right now, I'm going to throw this all over you.

GORDON. Christ you're sexy when you're angry.

ANGELA *throws the wine over* GORDON.

ANGELA. Tell. No-one.

She exits. GORDON *calls after her drunkenly.*

GORDON. I'm the Operational Manager, I can do what I like.
I'm putting it on expenses! All of it!

He wipes the wine off his face.

He raises an arm of greeting to a nearby table.

Hello.

*He notices the wedding ring on his hand and all of a
sudden the fight seems to go out of him.*

*He takes it off in one easy movement and drops it into his
empty wine glass.*

Then he slumps back in his chair.

9.

The large office after hours.

GRACE *with* DAMIEN. DAMIEN *getting ready to go home.*

GRACE. One of us might get to go on the telly.

DAMIEN. I doubt that.

GRACE. We might.

DAMIEN. It won't come to that, the police know what she's
like same as we do. She'll turn up.

GRACE. You don't seem very bothered about this.

DAMIEN. Grace, she's been my case for five years.

GRACE. She could be anywhere.

DAMIEN. She's not anywhere.

GRACE. I just think you should be taking this a bit more
seriously.

DAMIEN. Finish your Diploma. Leave the rest to me.

Pause. GRACE *is hurt.*

I'm sorry, that sounded harsher than I meant it to.

GRACE. S'okay.

DAMIEN. No look –

GRACE. No really it's fine.

DAMIEN. All I meant was –

GRACE. Talking of my course actually, I need a quick signature off you.

DAMIEN. Oh. Okay.

GRACE *produces some papers.*

GRACE. These are – well, I have to keep like a journal thing, you know, self-assessment, all that business.

DAMIEN. Yes, preparing you for bureaucracy.

GRACE. Well . . .

DAMIEN. God, I'm sounding such a cynic tonight. I'm sorry, I'm tired.

GRACE. It's fine.

DAMIEN. Give us a look.

GRACE. It's a sort of personal statement thing – reflections – and – and –

DAMIEN. Where do I sign?

GRACE. It's case notes and evaluations and stuff I've observed and –

DAMIEN. Just here?

GRACE. No look, you have to read it first –

DAMIEN. Ah, I'm sure it's fine –

GRACE. No I'd like you to –

DAMIEN. I've got to get off –

GRACE. Please.

DAMIEN. The childminder's only paid till seven –

GRACE. Just this week's then.

DAMIEN. I don't have my glasses –

GRACE. I'll read it to you. This is Monday's.

GRACE *snatches the papers from him.*

DAMIEN. Grace, please, / I can't fault your enthusiasm but it's the end of the day.

GRACE (*reading*). 'Child B, girl aged 15. In care since age 9. Family well-known to Department. Despite displaying early talent as a car mechanic, Child B is beyond control from age 12. Trashes office loo, attacks residential home staff, nearly kills herself with crack cocaine –

DAMIEN. Grace –

GRACE. 'Tuesday 29th – Child B absconds after prison visit to see father. Keyworker reluctant to contact police.

DAMIEN. Grace –

GRACE. 'Dilemma: we have a statutory duty to protect this child but at what cost to the trust established –

DAMIEN. Grace, you really don't have to –

GRACE. 'Thursday 1st – Child B missing for 48 hours, police considering appeal via local media. Personal dilemma: suspicion that keyworker-stroke-*mentor* knows of Child B's whereabouts –

DAMIEN. Grace for God's sake –

GRACE. 'Keyworker appears to believe own personal skills sufficient to somehow 'save' Child B from herself –

DAMIEN. Come on, that's / enough, show's over –

GRACE. ' – perhaps the manifestation of a *need* to be *needed* –

DAMIEN. Stop it now.

GRACE. ' – but in breaching the boundaries of his role, keyworker is jeopardising welfare of Child B.

DAMIEN. That's enough!

GRACE. 'Meanwhile concerns for Child B's safety escalating by the hour –

DAMIEN. Grace!

GRACE. 'Dilemma: What the fuck do I do?'

Pause.

DAMIEN. You want me to sign that do you?

Pause.

Grace if you want to discuss something, you only have to ask.

GRACE. And when are you ever free Damien?

DAMIEN. There is no need to do it like this.

Pause.

GRACE. Where is she?

DAMIEN. I have to get home.

GRACE. What level would this get you?

DAMIEN. It's my son's birthday.

GRACE. Verbal warning? Written? Full disciplinary?

Beat.

DAMIEN. I have a wife and child.

GRACE. And you'd protect *them* wouldn't you?

Pause.

DAMIEN. Do you drive?

GRACE. What?

DAMIEN. If you ever need any spare parts, there's a wrecker's yard on Amersham Way.

DAMIEN *hands* GRACE *the wrecker's yard's business card from Scene Three.*

They do quite a range. Bought a carburetter last time I was there. And between you and me, I don't own a car.

DAMIEN *grabs his truck and goes.* GRACE *examines the card.*

10.

GORDON*'s office, morning.*

DAWN *with* GORDON. GORDON *drinks coffee and wears the same suit from the restaurant.*

DAWN *holds some files.*

DAWN. What – and that's it?

GORDON. Those are the year's budgets. At least now you know the limits.

DAWN. Stand-still funding. Again. That's *completely* unrealistic.

GORDON. Dawn, the council's decided. Education and Health get the increases.

DAWN. As ever.

GORDON. Yes, as ever. Parks and Gardens also put in a strong bid this year.

DAWN. Good God.

GORDON. I don't like it any more than you do.

DAWN *holds a file up.*

DAWN. Okay, tell me where we're going to put Chloe.

GORDON. Sorry, Chloe . . . ?

DAWN. Chloe Fanshawe. Here. Angela's autistic kid. Mainstream can't deal with her, she needs 24 hour one-to-one care.

GORDON. Put it back to Education, it's their department.

DAWN. She was *referred* from Education.

GORDON. And what have Health said?

DAWN. Health – as always – don't want to know.

GORDON. Dawn, I don't decide these things. What about a private tutor? Short-term.

DAWN. Gordon, she's autistic. Change terrifies her, she hits the roof if there's too many pink ones in her liquorice allsorts.

GORDON. Give her to the Disability Team.

DAWN. She's a child, not a disease.

Beat.

GORDON. Dawn. You have to believe me. I put in the best bid possible for your team.

DAWN. Our team.

GORDON. Our team. Under the circumstances.

DAWN. What 'circumstances'?

Beat.

GORDON. Under-achievement.

DAWN. What?

GORDON. Consistent failure to meet the closure targets.

DAWN. Oh, the bloody government initiative.

GORDON. Yes. It's important.

DAWN. Is it?

GORDON. Yes.

DAWN. Okay. Chloe Fanshawe's case is hardly going to reach 'closure' if the kid's wreaking havoc all day at home.

GORDON. Look. The way you reach these targets . . . be flexible.

DAWN. What do you mean?

GORDON. Chloe is a case in point because we've picked it up now, but in future, you have to be stricter in accepting these referrals. If we don't accept a case, it isn't there to be closed.

DAWN. Hang on –

GORDON. Likewise with the classifications – if you identify fewer 'child in need' cases then there's fewer cases in the area and we're doing a better job. Whoever assesses the need has to take the case on and find the cash. I'm sorry, I don't like it any more than you but my hands are tied. If we're not seen to be improving we will always be passed over in the annual core funding increases. Intervene less, close early and you'll get the funding for all the future Chloe's that come your way. Assess more harshly, Dawn. Simple as that.

DAWN. I can't believe you're suggesting this.

GORDON *(shrugs)*. Desperate times.

DAWN. I'm sorry, I will *not* refuse to intervene in situations of serious actual or potential risk –

GORDON. I'm not asking you to – *obviously* in those cases you intervene, *obviously.* But elsewhere . . . just think twice.

Beat.

DAWN. These 'initiatives'. From on high. They just don't get it do they?

GORDON. Of course not. What do the government know?

DAWN. These aren't *police* files – these aren't *crime* cases that can be 'solved'.

GORDON. I know this.

DAWN. I mean – if – if there's an increase in *fires*, no-one blames *firemen*. Do they?

GORDON. Well, no.

DAWN. Or docks their funding. Can you *imagine*?

GORDON. I couldn't agree more.

DAWN. Gordon – it's a fundamental misunderstanding of the nature of our work.

GORDON. I *know*.

DAWN. And something needs to be said.

GORDON. Well . . . I have tried.

DAWN. We are about long-term cyclical intervention –

GORDON. Dawn, you're preaching to the converted. But what can we do?

DAWN. You tell me. I've got teenage girls running round out there in breach of licence because we reneged on our commitment – in court – to fund one on one staff! I've got private care homes charging me two grand a week – per child! I've got trainees working overtime for nothing! Zilch, no pay – nothing. What do they think we run this place on? Goodwill? Smiles? Something's got to give, Gordon. And I'm damned if it's going to be my professional integrity. My team are protecting almost 200 kids in this Borough. That means you are too. Give us what we need.

GORDON. Just . . . calm down. I have every faith in you. Here.

GORDON *gestures at the files* DAWN *is holding.*

DAWN. What?

GORDON. Give those to me.

DAWN. What, these?

GORDON. Yes. Come on. Who have we got?

He rifles through them.

Chloe we know about. Scott Henley . . .

DAWN. Rehab placement.

GORDON. Ali Beddows . . .

DAWN. Adoption breakdown.

GORDON. Surinder Jennings . . .

DAWN. We're prosecuting the stepdad.

GORDON. Fine. These are the most pressing?

DAWN. The most complicated. They're all inter-agency so
nothing's happening.

GORDON. Leave them with me.

DAWN. What are you going to do?

GORDON. Whatever I can. I'll get onto Alan in Health, Jess at
the drug place, and DCI what's-his-name. Get things
moving. Arrange some compromise. Alan and I play squash.

DAWN. Gordon –

GORDON. Trust me. I'll take care of it. Maybe you should
knock off a bit early today.

DAWN. I'm chairing a Child Protection Conference. Then I've
got a wedding reception.

GORDON. Oh. Good. Well. Try and have fun.

DAWN. Thanks. We'll catch up in the week.

GORDON. Naturally.

Beat. DAWN *points to a stained patch on* GORDON's
jacket pocket.

DAWN. There's something on your jacket.

GORDON. Oh. Thanks.

DAWN *goes.*

GORDON *puts the files in a drawer.*

He examines the stain on his jacket.

He takes a pack of melted butter out of the pocket.

GORDON. Shit.

11.

Quiet corner of a wedding reception, music from off.

DAWN *with* GRACE *and* ADELE.

ADELE *wears a wedding dress.* GRACE *and* ADELE *drink champagne,* DAWN *sips at a mineral water.*

Confetti hearts litter the floor and surfaces.

ADELE (*to* DAWN). Thank you so much for coming.

DAWN. Not at all, it's been lovely.

GRACE. Gorgeous dress.

ADELE (*bashful*). Oh. Thanks.

DAWN. Nothing like the meringue Gracie here described to me.

GRACE. Hey.

ADELE. We changed it. Tony and I. Last minute panic.

Pause. They drink.

Look Dawn, this might not be the time or the place – but sod it it's my bash – and I just wanted to say that I'm sorry. If I caused any friction.

DAWN. No, really.

ADELE. No I am. With the invites and so on. It was all a bit mad and – and rushed – and I – I wasn't thinking.

DAWN. Really, it's fine.

ADELE. Really?

DAWN. Really. It's my stuff, not yours.

ADELE. Okay. Thank you.

DAWN. Don't be silly.

Pause.

ADELE. Listen, there's aunties and uncles and – and people from *Ireland* and stuff, I should, er . . .

DAWN. Of course.

GRACE. Yeah, go on.

ADELE. I'll catch up with you a bit later maybe.

GRACE. Sure.

ADELE. Okay. And listen Dawn, give my love to Jenny, if
you . . . I mean if . . . actually, I'll probably see her before .
. . God, I'm really fucking up. I'm sorry I'm all a
bit . . . you know.

DAWN. It's fine.

ADELE. I'll go.

GRACE. Go on. Talk to the Irish.

ADELE. Right. Later.

DAWN. Yes.

ADELE. And thanks.

ADELE *goes.*

GRACE. Well.

DAWN. Yes. I'm sorry. That must have all been a bit . . .
mystifying.

GRACE. It's okay.

DAWN. Jenny . . . my daughter. You remember I was saying.
Her and Adele met travelling.

GRACE. Yes. Where is she? I'd love to meet her.

DAWN. Well, that's it you see. She's . . . we're . . . we're not
in touch.

GRACE. Oh. I'm sorry.

DAWN. No, no. Long story. Anyway, we were both invited.
Jenny found out I'd be here and . . . well. That was that.

GRACE. Oh Dawn. I don't know what to say.

DAWN. It's fine.

GRACE. Is it?

DAWN. No. Not really.

GRACE. Hey.

GRACE *hugs* DAWN. DAWN *manages not to cry.*

Sorry . . . was that . . . ?

DAWN. No. Thank you.

Pause.

Anyway.

GRACE. Yeah.

DAWN. Here we are.

GRACE. Yeah. Small world. Sure I can't get you a champers?

DAWN. I'm fine. I have a . . . a stomach thing. Booze doesn't help.

GRACE. Oh. Right.

DAWN. So. How are you finding things?

GRACE. Oh alright. I don't really want to talk about work. If that's alright.

DAWN. Of course. Sensible girl.

GRACE. Well.

DAWN. Everyone's enjoying having you there anyway.

GRACE. Oh. Good.

DAWN. New blood. Always refreshing.

GRACE. I'm glad.

DAWN. It's more than that though. You're good. You're very good. We get these trainees sometimes and . . . well. I'm sure you've heard the stories.

GRACE. Recruitment crisis.

DAWN. Tell me about it. What choice do we have?

Pause. DAWN *picks up a confetti heart.*

These are cute.

GRACE. Yeah.

DAWN. Here.

DAWN *throws a handful over* GRACE.

Souvenir.

GRACE. Get off! I'll be finding them for months!

They laugh and brush themselves down.

DAWN. Listen, Grace . . .

GRACE. Mm?

DAWN. You know, don't you, that – . . . I wanted you to know that . . . when you finish. The Diploma.

GRACE. Yes.

DAWN. There's a job for you. With us. As soon as you want it. *If* you want it.

GRACE. Wow. Thank you.

DAWN. But I don't know how long I'll be . . . I might not be . . . well. It'd be great to have you on board.

GRACE. Cool. We'll wait and see if I pass, eh?

DAWN. Don't be silly.

GRACE. I just might . . . I might need you to sign my report. At the end of the placement.

DAWN. Damien does all that.

GRACE. I just might need *you* to do that for me. I'd like you to.

DAWN. Oh. I understand.

GRACE. Yes.

Pause.

DAWN. Everything okay?

GRACE. Fine. Hey I've been meaning to ask you. If you can't answer this no-one can.

DAWN. Oh yeah?

GRACE. Have you found a tried and tested way to get work out of your head? Our work particularly I mean. The . . . bad stuff.

DAWN. Good question kiddo. If you find a way, let me know.

Pause.

You alright?

GRACE. Yeah. Just wondering.

DAWN. There's counselling courses if –

GRACE. Oh no. It's nothing like that.

DAWN. Well. If you're sure. Personally, I'm banking on retirement.

GRACE. Huh. Well tonight, I'm banking on drinking.

GRACE *drains her glass.*

Drinking and dancing. The old ways are best. Come on. There's a dancefloor over there.

GRACE *starts to go then holds out a hand to* DAWN.

DAWN (*smiles*). I'll watch.

She follows.

12.

DAWN*'s office, morning.*

DAWN *with* ANGELA.

ANGELA. I'll stand, thanks.

DAWN. Fine. Now, I wanted to have a bit of a chat about –

GRACE *enters.*

GRACE. Hi – oh, sorry. I'll pop back –

DAWN. No no, what's up?

GRACE. Just a quickie actually – the receipts for the go-karting? With Scott.

DAWN. Expenses form, here.

DAWN *hands* GRACE *a form.*

GRACE. Cool. Cheers.

GRACE *exits.*

DAWN. Now. Chloe Fanshawe.

ANGELA. Yes.

DAWN. Needs a place at the autism school.

ANGELA. Special school.

DAWN. Whatever. You know that I've spoken to her parents.

ANGELA. So have I.

DAWN. So you know the situation.

ANGELA. Can I just say, actually, how I think we need to get our priorities straight here – because we're denying a place for this kid at Mayfields due to lack of funds when we're perfectly happy to spend thousands of quid on – on that Star Trek thing –

DAWN. GPS –

ANGELA. Whatever – and – and take Scott Henley – of all people – out for a day's *go-karting* at the taxpayer's expense. I mean *come on.*

DAWN. You're talking about a forty quid day out for one our most at-risk youngsters, versus a forty *grand* placement – *per term* – at a special school fifty miles away.

ANGELA. I just don't see how we can *not* do it.

DAWN. Angela – I have begged and pleaded with Gordon over this one, I promise you. The only possibility is tri-partite funding if Health and Education come on board before the start of the new term.

ANGELA. Well they'd better do.

DAWN. Gordon's looking into it.

ANGELA. What's happening?

DAWN. Not much.

ANGELA. Well what a surprise that is.

DAWN. Well. None of that's really the issue here.

ANGELA. Oh. So what is?

DAWN. Angela, Chloe's parents –

ANGELA. John and Margaret, yes.

DAWN. Funny sort aren't they?

ANGELA. They're very vocal in their opinions, yes. I wouldn't describe them as funny.

DAWN. Funny peculiar, that is, not funny ha-ha.

ANGELA. I should hope not.

DAWN. It's just that – I don't know if you know this – but they've been bringing pressure to bear on a number of senior managers regarding this school place –

ANGELA. Or lack of.

DAWN. By making their feelings known to Gordon – amongst others I should add – by ringing him up.

ANGELA. Which they have every right to do.

DAWN. Several times a day.

ANGELA. Well his direct line's in the public domain.

DAWN. At home.

Pause.

You wouldn't know anything about this at all? Would you?

ANGELA. No. I wouldn't.

DAWN. I see. You wouldn't have any idea how they came to acquire the home telephone number of the Operational Manager?

ANGELA. No idea at all. That is *terrible*, isn't it? Poor Gordon. They might catch him in the middle of something.

Beat. Both smile, smiles become giggles.

DAWN. Don't. Don't start.

ANGELA. What? I didn't say a thing.

DAWN. Ange, please.

ANGELA. He *is* very active. Gordon. In his private life. Isn't he?

DAWN. I wouldn't know. Look, stop it.

ANGELA. Poor thing.

DAWN. Ssh, we mustn't. Save it for the Christmas party.

ANGELA. God help him.

DAWN. God help *us*.

ANGELA. Watch out Grace.

DAWN. Baptism of fire.

ANGELA. The coming of age!

They laugh.

DAWN. Coming of age! Oh stop it, we mustn't, we mustn't, ssh.

ANGELA. I'm sorry, I'm sorry.

Beat.

DAWN. Oh Ange. I don't wanna fight you any more. I don't wanna be your headmistress.

ANGELA. No. Save that for Gordon.

DAWN. Stop it.

ANGELA. Alright, alright.

DAWN. I can't keep coming after you, kiddo. I just don't have the energy. Just . . . behave. Please. And watch your back. You *will* get disciplined over stuff like that, the phone thing.

ANGELA. I'm just . . . I'm getting things done. My way.

DAWN. Which is fine. But not if it impacts on me. And the rest of the team. Please. It's not fair.

ANGELA. Alright.

DAWN. I have every sympathy with what you do. But it can't go on like this. One day I might not be here.

ANGELA. Sure. Thank you for the warning.

DAWN. Look out for yourself.

   DAWN*'s phone rings. She lets it ring for a moment.*

ANGELA. He's failed us both. In different ways. Hasn't he?

   A moment. Then DAWN *answers the phone.*

DAWN (*into phone*). Hello, Family Support.

   They smile at each other. ANGELA *goes.*

13.

SHIRLEY*'s retirement party at her house after work, suburban with a small garden.*

The lounge. ANGELA *with* GORDON *at the punch bowl.*

ANGELA *drinks punch from a glass.* GORDON *smokes.*

ANGELA. You know I'm leaving early.

GORDON. No.

ANGELA. Driving to Manchester.

GORDON. Oh.

ANGELA. Adam Leith's turned up at his auntie's.

GORDON. Oh yes of course. Sorry. Good luck.

ANGELA. Thanks.

Pause.

I'm staying with –

DAWN *enters carrying a huge salad bowl.*

DAWN. Sorry, don't mind me.

She squeezes between them.

Think we might be ready soon.

GORDON. Right.

DAWN *exits with salad to the garden.*

Sorry, what were you saying?

ANGELA. I'm staying with Jeff.

GORDON. Right. Who's that?

ANGELA. An old friend.

GORDON. Right.

ANGELA. An ex. From way back.

GORDON. Right. Why are you telling me this?

ANGELA. I thought you should know.

GORDON. I see.

ANGELA. How do you feel about that?

GORDON. About what?

ANGELA. Gordon. How do you feel?

GORDON. It's fine. You can do what you like, Angela. What does it matter?

Beat. ANGELA *offers a glass.*

ANGELA. Punch?

*

The garden. SHIRLEY *tends the barbecue with an apron on.* DAWN *has put the salad on the table and joined her.*

DAWN *is sniffing a bowl of marinade.*

SHIRLEY. It all goes into a sort of sugar glaze on the heat.

DAWN. Gorgeous. You must write this down.

SHIRLEY. It's all in my head. It's Dominican.

DAWN. Of course. Oh Shirl. We're going to miss you, you know.

SHIRLEY. Oh come now.

DAWN. No we are. I certainly am.

SHIRLEY. Well. Thank you.

DAWN. So. What's it gonna be? Retirement on the beach?

SHIRLEY. I don't know. I have not been back for nearly fifty years.

DAWN. What?

SHIRLEY. And Roy has never been.

DAWN. Hang on, Shirl. You haven't been home in *fifty* years?

SHIRLEY. *This* is my home.

DAWN. No, of course, but I mean, I thought you had family there. And friends.

SHIRLEY. Oh, once upon a time.

DAWN. Don't you miss them?

SHIRLEY. Dawn, you have to understand. My mother left me here when she was deported. I was twelve. It would be a strange thing to do. Going back now.

DAWN. Of course. I'm sorry.

SHIRLEY. Imagine . . . imagine you were to see your daughter again. Like hacking open an old old scar. Yes?

DAWN (*quiet*). Yes.

SHIRLEY. Keep moving. Keep moving on.

A moment. Then GORDON *enters.*

GORDON. Ah-ha. Where the action is.

SHIRLEY. Sorry?

DAWN. Hello, Gordon.

GORDON (*to* SHIRLEY). May I?

SHIRLEY. If you wish.

> GORDON *takes the tongs from* SHIRLEY *and prods at the barbecue.*

GORDON. Lovely. This looks lovely.

DAWN. Shirley's done a special marinade.

GORDON. Ah-ha.

> *He sniffs it.*

Mmm, Jamaican. Lovely.

*

The kitchen. GRACE *with* DAMIEN. *They chop broccoli and speak in hushed tones.*

DAMIEN. What did she tell you?

> *Pause.*

Grace – is she at risk?

GRACE. I think so.

DAMIEN. Serious risk?

GRACE. Janine's always at serious risk.

DAMIEN. Grace. Look at me. You have to tell me.

> ANGELA *enters, drinking.*

ANGELA. Hey. How's it going?

DAMIEN. Fine.

GRACE. Yeah.

DAMIEN. Just doing . . . just doing broccoli.

ANGELA. Party on.

GRACE. Not laying the table?

ANGELA. They're managing. (*To* DAMIEN.) Hey, how did Charlie like his truck?

DAMIEN. It's too big for him. He can't work the controls.

ANGELA. Oh well. He'll grow into it.

GRACE (*to* DAMIEN). Yeah, hours of fun for *you* at least.

ANGELA *picks a confetti heart off the broccoli.*

ANGELA. There's something on this.

GRACE. Oh, sorry. Confetti heart. Went to a wedding and can't get rid of the bloody things.

ANGELA *finds a couple more.*

ANGELA. They're everywhere.

GRACE. Oh dear.

ANGELA. Nice little place this, isn't it?

DAMIEN. Yeah, I'd retire here.

ANGELA. That's a bit of a way off isn't it?

DAMIEN. Oh, I dunno.

GRACE (*mutters*). Gotta do some work first . . .

DAMIEN. I'm sorry?

GRACE. Hm?

ANGELA. Yeah, what did you say?

GORDON *calls from off.*

GORDON (*off*). It's ready!

GRACE. Oh no. Veggies aren't anywhere near. Ange, be a love would you? Go and tell them.

A moment, then ANGELA *goes.*

DAMIEN. What was that?

GRACE. What?

DAMIEN. Don't speak to me like that.

GRACE. Chill out, it was a joke.

DAMIEN. You're like an insolent child sometimes.

GRACE. I'll get myself a toy truck shall I?

DAMIEN. I'm not rising to that.

Beat.

Come on. What did you find out?

GRACE. Well. Janine's pregnant.

DAMIEN. Oh God.

GRACE. By Buddy.

DAMIEN. Oh shit.

GRACE. Who is also her pimp.

DAMIEN. What?

GRACE. He runs a prostitution racket with the wrecker's yard as a front. The girls are in the house next door, the deals are done in the front office. Don't tell me you didn't know this.

DAMIEN. Of course I bloody didn't.

GRACE. Suspected then.

DAMIEN. I've been *through* this with her. And she *insisted*. Are you *sure?*

GRACE. Of course I'm sure. I went to that yard and I asked her.

DAMIEN. Why didn't you tell me?

GRACE. I *am* telling you.

Pause.

I can't believe you've got the cheek to bollock me for this.

DAMIEN. I beg your pardon?

GRACE. You *knew* where she was.

DAMIEN. I was *dealing* with it. She trusts me.

GRACE. I'm sorry to break this to you Damien, but her feelings for you are far from affectionate.

DAMIEN. What, she told you this? Just like that?

GRACE. I don't think she likes men very much. Understandably.

DAMIEN. I was working on it. Grace, these things take time – weeks, *months*. You can't just go in there and –

GRACE. What? Protect her? Why can't I do that? You took your eye off the ball Damien. *Your* way didn't work.

Pause.

DAMIEN. Look, if you tell Dawn she'll –

DAWN. I know. And for all this mess, I don't want to do that to you.

DAMIEN. Right. Right. What shall we do?

GRACE. Christ, *I'm* the trainee!

DAMIEN. I'll talk to her.

GRACE. Dawn?

DAMIEN. Janine.

GRACE. You won't get very far.

DAMIEN. Please. I can find a way through this. I can.

Pause.

GRACE. Tomorrow – first thing. Go to the yard. I'm telling
Dawn we've found her at lunch time.

*

The garden.

GORDON *piles meat up on a dish. He wears the apron now.*

DAWN *and* SHIRLEY *set the table.*

ANGELA *stands with a glass of punch. She is drunk.*

ANGELA. Thirty years, yeah?

GORDON. I'm putting them back on, I think they need a bit
longer.

DAWN. Make your mind up.

SHIRLEY. Twenty-eight years, Angela.

ANGELA. Right well whatever, a long time right – a long time
in the same place.

SHIRLEY. Yes I know, I am a dinosaur –

DAWN. Oh no, more of a rare breed –

SHIRLEY. Well thank you. I think.

ANGELA. I just wondered Shirl, if you ever thought that your
predicament might be symptomatic.

SHIRLEY. Of what?

DAWN. Ange, go and chase the others up would you?

ANGELA. Of institutional racism.

Beat.

SHIRLEY. I beg your pardon?

DAWN. Ange please, we're really going to need that broccoli soon.

ANGELA. Because it's symptomatic isn't it? Of something far more pernicious than this little soirée would suggest. It's the glass ceiling, isn't it? The glass ceiling in action.

GORDON. You know Angela, I think I fancy that punch now.

ANGELA. I just thought it might be interesting to look at it as a possibility. Interesting for Gordon, as he's here. As he's very kindly dropped by. Useful for him. To delve into the sort of establishment he's running.

To unpack the issues really. Philosophically.

DAWN (*quiet*). Oh Angela. I thought we'd reached an understanding.

ANGELA. Would that be useful for you, Gordon?

SHIRLEY. Please. Why can't we leave all this in the office?

DAWN. Ange, please. No more.

ANGELA. I just thought this was an ideal opportunity. Informally. Such as we are.

SHIRLEY. This is my send off. We are all here to wish each other well.

ANGELA (*to* SHIRLEY). So you don't deny it then.

SHIRLEY. I stayed where I am through choice. I have lost count of the amount of times I have been asked to move into management, but each time I have declined. I like my own small patch of work, and I like to be left to get on with it. As much as I like my colleagues, I wish them to remain as my peers. Some of them, I would not like to have to manage. Sometimes, Angela, people are of a different race – and everything is alright. The problems start when we are constantly reminded how *different* we are to each other. Look at the children we deal with. Look at the little ones. What do they care about colour? They have to be taught. We have to be taught how to hate each other so much.

Pause.

ANGELA. I have to go. Adam needs me.

ANGELA exits.

DAWN. Ange, wait. Ange! She's not driving to Manchester in that state. Stay here.

DAWN exits. Pause.

GORDON. Bugger. I think these are burning.

14.

Greasy café, morning.

DAMIEN *with* JANINE. DAMIEN *holds a mobile phone.*

DAMIEN. Please. We've got three hours.

JANINE. You mean *you've* got three hours.

DAMIEN. Ring in now and say you went away –

JANINE. What?

DAMIEN. – but that you're fine and you're on your way back to the home and you're sorry.

JANINE. Why the hell should I do that?

DAMIEN. Because, Janine, you could go straight back to secure for this.

JANINE. For what?

DAMIEN. You've been missing for 72 hours!

JANINE. Only 'cos of *you!* I haven't *been* anywhere! Have I? You've just done fuck all about it!

Pause.

You're in trouble intcha?

DAMIEN. It's under control.

JANINE. And you want me to rescue you.

DAMIEN. What I *did,* Janine, was to try and safeguard a bond of trust between the two of us –

JANINE. Ha!

DAMIEN. – by not sending the police in to Buddy's yard, like I promised you.

JANINE. No, that's not it. You thought we were so pally, such great mates, that you'd swoop in like Superman –

DAMIEN. No!

JANINE. – and I'd come trotting out after ya like Lois Lane.

DAMIEN. That's not it at all.

JANINE. Well look at Superman now. Clark Kent's fell off his horse and he's fucked.

DAMIEN. That's Christopher Reeves, Clark Kent was the character –

JANINE. And he ain't never gonna get better.

DAMIEN. Apparently he's making progress.

JANINE. Well then he's doing better than you.

DAMIEN. Look! I am not here to talk about Superman!

JANINE. Damien, I am *fine*. I'm getting by, earning money, looking out for meself, getting on with my life. Why don't you do the same?

DAMIEN. What?

JANINE. You heard.

DAMIEN. Don't pretend you know anything about my life.

JANINE. Don't I? I've had loads like you. You're all the same. Your tank tops and your Volvos and your knight-in-shining-armour routine.

DAMIEN. Janine, please –

JANINE. I mean why the *fuck* do you do this job eh?

DAMIEN. I don't even own a tank top.

JANINE. I mean, why would you fuckin *bother?*

DAMIEN. Or a Volvo.

JANINE. Good! 'Cos they're shit!

DAMIEN. Look, these things are hardly the issue here!

JANINE. I mean what do you know about how I've lived? How fuckin hard has your life been?

DAMIEN. Listen to yourself, Janine. You're articulate, bright – *angry*. Think what you could do with that.

JANINE. Oh yeah, I could ponce off and be some fuckin *lawyer* or summing.

DAMIEN. Yeah, if that's what you want.

JANINE. I'm happy where I am.

DAMIEN. Oh what, you really want the pinnacle of your life's achievements to be working as a prostitute?

JANINE. *I* am a mechanic.

Beat.

DAMIEN. Until you take responsibility for your situation, you're not going to get anywhere.

JANINE. I just wanna be left alone.

DAMIEN. What most people don't realise Janine, especially when they're growing up –

JANINE. I *am* grown up.

DAMIEN. – is that you can be anything you want in life. Anything at all. Rocket scientist, brain surgeon, Formula One driver – whatever. You just have to *want* it enough.

JANINE. Then why haven't *you* managed to be a social worker?

Pause.

DAMIEN. I did my best for you.

JANINE. Oh yeah?

DAMIEN. Yeah. Right here, in this place you're at now, I might be your only friend.

JANINE. Don't turn that one on me. *I* might be *yours*.

Pause.

Look, what do you wanna do? I mean really.

DAMIEN. What?

JANINE. You're not cut out for this. What about that thing you're always goin on about? With little kids.

DAMIEN. What . . . play therapy?

JANINE. Yeah. Go and do that. You might be quite good at that.

DAMIEN. I'm quite good at *this*.

JANINE. Damien. You can be whatever you wanna be. You just have to *want* it enough. Innit.

DAMIEN *sniffs*.

Oh fuckin hell. Don't *cry* on me.

15.

Small flat in Manchester, New Age décor.

Leftovers from a meal for two.

ANGELA *and* JEFF *having after-dinner drinks,* ANGELA *smokes a spliff.*

JEFF *Manchester accent, dreadlocks, rolls another.*

ANGELA. And his *mother* right – God I hate her, the bitch – his *mother* only goes and tells him in hospital doesn't she?

JEFF. That's heavy shit.

ANGELA. Fucking tell me about it. So it's suddenly clear to the poor kid why his Dad's been such a non-entity for the past two years – his *Dad,* who's now *not* his Dad any more –

JEFF. How old is he?

ANGELA. Fifteen. I mean if she'd just *worked* with us 'stead of bloody fighting us every step of the way – I mean he'd have to have found out soon anyway, he's getting to that age –

JEFF. Sorry – you got anything I can roach?

ANGELA. Yeah, hang on.

ANGELA *rummages in her bag.*

She unearths various things, including the GPS handset from Scene Five.

ANGELA. But anyway, she has to go over our heads and whack him with it in *hospital* – I mean *hospital* of all places – recovering from a fucking overdose. I mean no wonder the poor kid's off his head all the time smashing and burning shit, no fucking wonder – I mean the mind boggles that you've got parents out there that can –

JEFF. Finish the bottle?

ANGELA. Yeah cheers.

JEFF *tops them up. He notices the GPS.*

JEFF. What's that?

ANGELA (*still rummaging*). Oh, a – you know, one of those –
it's a Star Trek thing, tells the office where I am.

JEFF. Oh. Why?

ANGELA. I dunno. Protection. So anyway the call comes in
from the police that he's nicked off from the ward and
they're all out there – 'cos we sort of do that, sort of let the
police do the running around – and 'course the first place
they look is round his foster parents, and of course he
wasn't there, but d'ya know what they found?

JEFF. He hadn't burned it down again had he?

ANGELA. No, worse. A torn up guinea pig.

JEFF. What?

ANGELA. He had this guinea pig. Harold or Harvey or
something. Dad got it him for his birthday. Tore it up.

JEFF. What –

ANGELA. Yeah.

JEFF. You mean like –

ANGELA. Yeah. Legs, head, tore it up.

JEFF. Oh, man.

ANGELA. I know.

JEFF. A real guinea pig?

ANGELA. Yup.

JEFF. That is . . . fucked.

ANGELA. This is not a happy child.

JEFF. God, I can't get it out of me head.

ANGELA. So thank fuck I mean thank *fuck* he turns up here –
he's got an auntie here or summing – 'cos he's fifteen and –
and – and despite everything – two years of working with
the kid and he's still out of control. It's useless.

JEFF. Oh mate. 'Course it's not. Stoppin em getting *worse* –
that's progress int it?

ANGELA. Well. Thanks. Here.

ANGELA *has found what she was looking for and hands*
JEFF *the legislative document that* DAWN *gave her in*
Scene One.

JEFF. Cheers.

JEFF *begins tearing it up for the spliff.*

What *is* this?

ANGELA. Children Act 1989. Anyway, next morning – like
this morning – there's the letter. And it's all there. The
abuse. *Years* of sexual abuse from the maternal grandfather.
Anyway, that's how it all comes out isn't it, in arson and
pill-popping and – and – and fucking *pet* murder. I mean
I .believe him, frankly I believe him, it explains so much.
But Dawn right, Dawn, that's the bald one, she's alright
when you get to know her is Dawn, anyway *Dawn* reckons
it's revenge tactics from Adam – sorry, shouldn't mention
names, you didn't hear that –

JEFF. Yeah, man.

ANGELA. *She* reckons it's malicious to get at Jackie for –

JEFF. That's the Mum?

ANGELA. That's the Mum – to get at Jackie for the revelation
about the affair. I mean you couldn't fuckin *make* it up.

JEFF. But I mean Ange, right – how are you gonna convince
him to go back down with ya?

ANGELA. Oh I've got his number. I'll talk him round. Don't
worry about it. This is what I do.

JEFF. You have a mad job.

ANGELA. Fuckin *tell* me about it.

JEFF. No I don't mean it bad, like. Stressbag, man. You gotta
learn to let it go.

ANGELA. How? You tell me how. My life's not me own.

Pause.

JEFF. It's good to see ya.

ANGELA. Yeah, you too baby. It's been too long hasn't it?

JEFF. Yeah. Life gets in the way don't it?

ANGELA *yawns.*

ANGELA. God, I'm suddenly wasted.

JEFF *takes the spliff off her.*

JEFF. Hey. You've got a hell of a day tomorrow. I made up the spare room.

ANGELA. Oh, you're lovely.

JEFF. Might smell of paint a bit, had all me materials in there.

ANGELA. Oh and you moved them all? For me? Ah, Jeffy.

JEFF. S'alright.

ANGELA. God. I've whinged on about work all night haven't I? I'm sorry. How's things with you?

JEFF. It's alright. Yeah it's alright. Exhibition and that comin up. Sold a few.

ANGELA. Ah nice one. Good for you. Yeah this kid paints a bit. He's good, been trying to encourage him.

JEFF. Hey Ange.

ANGELA. What?

JEFF. Forget about him.

ANGELA. Oh. Yeah. God I'm so sorry.

JEFF. It's alright man. You should crash. Chill out an that.

ANGELA. Yeah.

Pause.

You, er, you hitting the sack?

JEFF. Yeah. Y'alright for T-shirts an that?

ANGELA. Yeah. Don't wear anything these days. Au naturelle, you know.

JEFF. Right. I'll er – I'll –

ANGELA. Jeff.

JEFF. What?

ANGELA. I've been screwing my boss.

JEFF. Oh.

Pause.

Not that bald woman?

ANGELA. No. *Her* boss.

JEFF. Oh.

ANGELA. And it's a disaster. Everything's just a disaster.

JEFF. Oh dear.

ANGELA. I'm gonna have to quit. (*Tearful.*) I'm gonna have to quit my job.

JEFF. Is it that bad?

ANGELA. Yeah. I don't know what I was thinking of. We're chalk and cheese. He's my complete opposite. He's *your* complete opposite. I hate him. There's just something . . . animal there. I can't stop fucking him.

Pause.

ANGELA. How do you feel about that?

JEFF. Erm. Well. It's a pity it's gone that far. Innit.

ANGELA. I mean, how do you *feel*?

JEFF. I don't get ya.

ANGELA. Does it make you jealous?

JEFF. Oh. No. Not any more.

ANGELA. Oh.

Pause.

Jeff?

JEFF. Yeah?

ANGELA. Can I . . . can I come in with you tonight?

Pause.

JEFF. Ange . . .

ANGELA. Just like we used to. Just like old times.

JEFF. Ange, I can't.

ANGELA. Jeff. Make love to me. Tonight. Please.

JEFF. Ange. It's not like that now. It's not. Stuff's . . . changed. I'm sorry.

ANGELA *begins to cry, quietly.*

ANGELA. Then just . . . just love me. Please.

JEFF *goes to her, hesitantly.* ANGELA *clutches him.*

JEFF. Hey. Ange. Ange, man.

ANGELA. I can't do it anymore. I can't do it. Every day . . . all the time . . . the knives are out . . . and I just . . . I just don't have the strength.

JEFF. Hey. C'mon. You're the strongest I've ever met. If you can't do it, no-one can.

ANGELA *continues to cry.*

JEFF. One last time.

ANGELA. What?

JEFF. For this boy. Tomorrow.

ANGELA. Oh.

JEFF. You're all he's got.

ANGELA. Just love me, Jeff. Just love me.

Beat.

JEFF. I do love you, Ange. I do.

16.

DOCTOR*'s surgery.*

DAWN *with* DOCTOR. DAWN *has her head scarf off for the first time. Her hair is patchy and thin. The* DOCTOR *has just finished examining her.*

DOCTOR. It's rare, but not as rare as people imagine. Something like two per cent of the population will get it at some time in their lives.

DAWN. How funny. That's the same percentage that meet people like me. There's a thesis in there somewhere.

DOCTOR. I doubt it's related.

DAWN. It was a joke.

DOCTOR. I see. Well. No-one knows why it happens. Stress of modern life, perhaps.

DAWN. So it *is* stress-related.

DOCTOR. No-one's quite sure. Something triggers the
immune system to attack the hair follicles but no-one's quite
sure what. But either way, stress isn't going to help is it?

DAWN. No. I suppose not.

DOCTOR. Your stomach ulcer, whilst of course less visible, is
more worrying.

DAWN. Yes.

DOCTOR. You have high stress levels in your job.

DAWN. Yes.

DOCTOR. But you're close to retirement.

DAWN. Well. Five years.

DOCTOR. Can you take it early?

DAWN. No – I – No. I can't.

DOCTOR. I see.

DAWN. My work – it's just . . . I can't.

DOCTOR. Ms. Talbot. Learning to devolve responsibility will
be the first step towards lowering the stress levels in your
life.

DAWN. I can't do that. I'm sorry. It's . . . you wouldn't
understand.

DOCTOR. Well. In that case. There's a limit to what we can
do for you.

DAWN. Anyway. Look. I have to get off. What can you give
me?

The DOCTOR *writes.*

DOCTOR. I'm prescribing a course of Cortisone injections.
It's the most common treatment for your form of Alopecia.
You'll need to see a dermatologist once a month who will
inject directly into the bare patches in your scalp. It doesn't
combat the disease but it does stimulate the hair follicles to
grow again. At the very least it should protect you from
further damage.

DAWN. Alopecia.

DOCTOR. Yes.

DAWN. Funny word.

DOCTOR. Alopecia Areata is the form you have. It's the most common.

DAWN. Alopecia. Sounds like somewhere you might go on holiday, doesn't it? 'I'm off to Alopecia.' 'I'm retiring to Alopecia.'

Pause.

I thought I might retire to Greece.

DOCTOR. Yes. Well. The sooner the better in my opinion.

DAWN. Retire to Greece and practise Aromatherapy. Reflexology. Massage. I expect you hate all that don't you?

DOCTOR. We try to keep an open mind. I trained as a physiotherapist once upon a time.

DAWN. Really. I wanted to be an actress. Funny how things turn out.

Pause. The DOCTOR *hands* DAWN *her prescription.* DAWN *puts her head scarf on.*

17.

Amusement arcade.

ANGELA *with* ADAM *at a games machine.* ADAM *shoots at the screen with a plastic gun.*

ANGELA. Adam, stop that a minute.

ADAM. What?

ANGELA. Have you heard anything I've said?

ADAM. I'm on level six.

ANGELA. I'm trying to explain something to you.

ADAM. What? You're going on holiday. So what?

ANGELA. No. I'm going away.

ADAM. Where?

ANGELA. I don't know yet. I'm applying for VSO.

ADAM. You what?

ANGELA. Voluntary Service Overseas.

ADAM. What's that?

ANGELA. It's working abroad.

ADAM. Oh right. Like a summer job? My cousin did that. Picked cherries.

ANGELA. No, it's . . . ot quite the same. You get to – to teach English in Africa or – or build schools in Nicaragua or –

ADAM. Where's that?

ANGELA. Central America.

ADAM. Oh. That's quite far away int it?

ANGELA. Yes.

ADAM. How long's it take to do all that?

ANGELA. The minimum placement is two years.

ADAM. What?

ANGELA. I'm sorry.

ADAM. Two *years*? You mean two *months* dontcha? It's two months int it?

ANGELA. No.

Pause.

ADAM. You can't do that.

ANGELA. I'm sorry.

ADAM. Is it 'cos of the guinea pig?

ANGELA. No.

ADAM. The cat then.

ANGELA. No.

ADAM. 'Cos I failed art?

ANGELA. No. It's nothing to do with *you*. It's about me.

ADAM. Oh. What about me?

ANGELA. Oh Adam. Please, you have to understand. It's nothing you've said or done or –

ADAM. What do I do now?

ANGELA. Well. Um. You'll be re-allocated.

ADAM. What?

ANGELA. To a new worker.

Pause. ADAM *puts another 50p in the machine and starts playing.*

ANGELA. Adam.

ADAM *keeps playing.*

Adam listen to me.

ADAM. I've had to start again now. Level One. Look. It's shite.

ANGELA. I'm trying to say goodbye.

ADAM. Right. Bye then.

ANGELA. You'll be looked after. You will. You will.

ANGELA *goes.*

When she has gone, ADAM *stops playing.*

He picks something off the screen. A confetti heart.

18.

Split scene.

DAMIEN *on a chair facing an interview panel.*

ANGELA *on the telephone.*

GRACE *with a laptop, reading back her case notes from the screen.*

DAWN *at home, alone. She shaves her head with a straight razor.*

GORDON *delivering a speech.*

DAMIEN. I've been through the worst sorts of hell the job can offer. I've been sent shit and used condoms in the post. I've been attacked at three in the morning on a night shift in residential. I didn't hold it against him. I didn't press charges. Because you can't. Because with *those* kids, by the time they get to you, the damage is done.

ANGELA. Shirley? It's Angela. From work. Yes, yes it must be. It's been a little while hasn't it? Is this a good time?

How's a life of leisure treating you? Good. Oh good I'm
glad, you deserve it. *Grand*mother? My God, congratulations!

GRACE (*reading*). 'Child C. Boy aged 15 in local foster care.
Came down from the north aged 8 following mother and
new boyfriend. Disrupted family background – unstable
mother, violent father. Following move, mother immediately
decides she can't cope. Child C placed by Department in
children's home, as is usual practice.

GORDON. Good morning. I'd like to start by expressing my
excitement at taking up this position, and at being given the
privilege of taking forward the achievements of our
workforce at a strategic level – whilst also working in full
collaboration with the Social Services Committee of this
Council.

DAMIEN. Play Therapy – for me anyway – it's about bringing
out those things that are inside and putting them into the
real world in some way. Play is the natural form of
communication for a child. And we as adults need to play as
well, we all need to play.

ANGELA. Look, the reason I'm ringing – other than for a bit
of a catch-up – is that, uh, well, things have . . . taken a new
direction for me. No, I'm – I'm leaving. No don't start all
that it's the right thing – yes, oh yes don't worry. But I'm
off to do VSO.

GRACE. 'Contact arrangement irregular due to mother's
chaotic lifestyle. Father no fixed abode. Over the years,
behaviour becomes increasingly violent and disturbed. Kills
mother's cat. Tears up own guinea pig. Goes to special
school and hates it. Destroys his own art coursework shortly
before GCSE assessment.

GORDON. There are many challenges facing our Department,
there can be no doubt about that. The challenge of
continuing to protect our vulnerable children. Of effectively
implementing the government's policies of social inclusion.
Of forging effective inter–agency partnerships. Ensuring
that such positive dialogues remain meaningful. In the
interests of working in partnership to safeguard our clients.

DAMIEN. It's about giving children a – a safe space to do that
– and just sort of playing out issues really. If you play it out
then it's a little bit less that's inside you. And this is where

you get children who are destructive, because these things aren't being channelled in a safe way.

GRACE. 'Mother discloses that Child C is not his father's son, but the result of affair with boss during temping job in the eighties. News sends Child C over the edge.

DAMIEN. So they're not managing at school or – or they're running away all the time.

GRACE. Absconds to auntie's in Manchester.

DAMIEN. And they don't recognise this, how can they? That's our job.

GRACE. 'Alleges years of sexual abuse from maternal grandfather.

GORDON. These are challenges to which I – and indeed all of us here today – must not fail to rise.

GRACE. 'Police investigation opens.

GORDON. But one thing I *shall* stress now is this: the importance of being funded and resourced properly to do our job.

GRACE. 'Maternal grandfather arrested on Christmas Eve.

GORDON. We *must* ensure we meet the government's case closure targets in order to bring in this new money. To fail to do so would be to compromise every vulnerable child in this Borough.

DAMIEN. Anyway. This is the age you catch them, what you guys do here. I know I didn't finish the training but I – well, I had a little boy of my own, you know how it is.

ANGELA. Well you sort of get sent to the areas with greatest need. And of course it changes all the time.

DAMIEN. And he's wonderful, he's great.

ANGELA. But what I've landed up with is this sort of admin post running a community centre in – guess where?

DAMIEN. I just love playing with him, I love it.

ANGELA. Dominica, yeah!

DAMIEN. But I'm more than happy to put in the extra hours to catch up. Really, I am.

Distantly, a phone starts ringing. Lights down on DAMIEN.

ANGELA. Anyway, I thought I'd give you a ring and see – well, just see if you were around really. I thought we could have lunch and – and talk and practise our French and . . . and say goodbye.

Another phone starts ringing. Lights down on ANGELA.

GRACE. 'Child C's keyworker leaves the profession for personal reasons.

GORDON. I look forward to working with you all.

Another phone starts ringing. Lights down on GORDON.

GRACE. 'Child C allocated to new trainee.

A phone rings in DAWN*'s house.* DAWN *stops shaving her head and puts down the razor.*

She answers it. The other phones stop suddenly.

DAWN. Yes.

Pause.

Jenny? Oh God. Oh thank God.

Lights down on DAWN.

GRACE. 'Case status: Open.'

Fade to black.